The American Movie Goddess

Perception in Communication

GENERAL EDITOR
Charles Saunders

THE VOICES OF WAR
James Shokoff

MALE AND FEMALE: IDENTITY
John Harrington

ALIENATION: MINORITY GROUPS
Don Rude

WHO NEEDS NATURE?
Dixie Smith Jackson

THE AMERICAN MOVIE GODDESS
Marsha McCreadie

The American Movie Goddess

Edited by
MARSHA McCREADIE
University of Illinois at Urbana-Champaign

John Wiley & Sons, Inc.
New York
London
Sydney
Toronto

Library of Congress Cataloging in Publication Data:

McCreadie, Marsha, 1943-
The American movie goddess.

(Perception in communication series)
1. Moving-picture actors and actresses, American—Biography. 2. United States—Popular culture.
I. Title.

PN1998.A2M26 791.43'028'0922 72-14279
ISBN 0-471-58320-0

Printed in the United States of America

10 9 8 7 6 5 4 3 2 1

Series Preface

"Perception in Communication" is a series of brief topical readers presenting a collection of expository prose, verse, fiction, drama, and nonverbal media for the student of composition. No restrictive framework has been imposed on any of the volumes. If a common framework exists, it stems from the editors' emphasis on the principle of comparison and contrast and their mutual desire to make the questions and exercises participatory. The questions are focused on themes and matters of rhetorical technique that will provoke discussion between instructor and student in responses to the authors and editors.

Experience demonstrates that a student tends to write better when a timely, substantial subject engages his interest, or when the subject is elaborated and reviewed in a variety of modes of communication. Although the major emphasis of this series is on written communication, there are also a number of multimedia projects such as collages, comic routines, poems, dramatic productions, films, pictorial essays, posters, songs, and tapes. The editors use this multimedia material in such a manner that they are very definitely assignments in composition.

By acknowledging several modes of communication and encouraging experimentation in more than one, the editors recognize the heterogeneity of today's college audience and its various commitments, concerns, goals, and needs. It is the editors' belief that presenting these various modes of communication will engage not only the reader's mind but also his sensory perception.

CHARLES SANDERS
University of Illinois at Urbana

Preface

This book, designed for a freshman or sophmore course in writing, is a collection of photographs, essays, song lyrics, illustrations, and other material from three decades of recent American cultural history: the thirties, the forties, and the fifties. Some of the selections have not been previously published; some are famous and familiar; others are statements by noted writers and thinkers.

But the book is more than a compilation of nostalgic artifacts. I have presented the material in such a fashion that a theory or set of theories may be deduced: that particular images (as embodied in major female movie stars) were demanded by, foisted on, or evolved for the American public. These images can be observed in clothes, furniture, advertisements, or even in the buildings of each era; and they also may be an extension of popular beliefs which depended on such diverse matters as economics, political events, and prevailing social and sexual mores.

The movie stars discussed are Greta Garbo, Rita Hayworth, and Marilyn Monroe. These three stars may be a reflection of or a partial cause for the images created by the times, but the selection and my frequent comments do not lead to such a restrictive conclusion. Instead, the placement of material and my observations encourage the student to make his own summaries and to ask his own questions.

The book is divided into three parts, and there are questions and projects at the end of each section which encourage coherent thinking and writing. The basic topics of the book will undoubtedly interest the student; and the questions and projects are open-ended, involving research, personal interviews, design, film making and, of course, writing.

It is my hope that **The American Movie Goddess** *will encourage students and teachers to think in a more connective manner about the quality of American life: how the cultural phenomena that constantly surround us affect our emotions and, ultimately, our thoughts. Will a free hand at analysis, instead of a minute and cautious attempt, enlighten us about all those things that so obviously have formed and will continue to for our consciousness?*

These questions are explored, and the student is prompted to ask additional ones.

MARSHA McCREADIE
Urbana, Illinois, 1973

Contents

THE FORTIES: THE EXOTIC BAD GIRL—PIN-UPS, MECHANIZED SEX, FUN, AND WAR

THE FIFTIES: BRINGING IT ALL HOME WITH THE INNOCENT-BLONDE, SYNTHETICALLY NATURAL SEX QUEEN

The American Movie Goddess

"Stars and Worshippers: Daydream or Nightmare?"

Looking for cause and effect in the cultural life of a nation is like the old riddle of the chicken and the egg. For example, does a movie star represent trends that are already present, or does he or she actually help create styles and ideas? The "representational" theory assumes that viewers identify most readily with what is familiar to them, or what they perhaps believe they themselves are. And the other "trend-setter" theory proves the old dictum about admiration—that imitation *is* the sincerest form of flattery. A corollary to both of these theories is that the movie theater is a kind of dream-state: the audience projects into, and gets vicarious pleasure from, a wish-fulfilling image or fantasy. Either of these approaches emphasizes the intimate connection between the movie star phenomenon and pop-cultural trends in social and sexual behavior, taste in clothing, art, furniture, and even attitudes about political and economic conditions.

Pauline Kael answers the question democratically: there is much the audience sees of itself, she says, and much it is educated to, but the ultimate choice is left open—the viewer can accept or reject those images on the screen. Marshall McLuhan takes a possibly more frightening view of taste creation: as in advertising, the Hollywood producer attempts to analyze and keep alive certain myths the viewer will be unable to resist. This insidious mind-bending explains cultism and the large profits made from it.

But perhaps more fascinating and elusive than either of these culture-oriented theories is the familiar notion of movie stars as gods and goddesses. Those who see the star this way can account for fantasy-projection, adulation and worship, as well as the structure of Hollywood itself—with its sycophants and frustrated underlings. Jeans Cocteau, screenwriter and playwright, recognized the *Photoplay*-type cliché: "The cinema, that temple of sex, with its goddesses, its guardians and its victims."

The gods and goddesses are always the Adonis–Aphrodite type, and often they come to "pay for" their exceptional glory and beauty. Alexander Walker, a British movie critic, sees especially the female movie-star role in this way (Diana Trilling, an American cultural analyst, agrees that this is so, particularly in the case of Marilyn Monroe). It is, of course, true that many of the lives of the movie goddesses turn out to be tragic; one might even conjecture that it is the American Puritan conscience (implementing the anthropological necessity of god-sacrifice for a society) that insists on punishing its heroes and heroines after vicariously enjoying their roles and lives.

These three approaches, each one perhaps more extreme than the others, offer some explanation of a phenomenon that has dominated the pop-cultural life of most of the American twentieth century. And the verbal and visual inclusions in this short volume are a small sampling of a constantly changing but recurring motif in our lives and the lives of the generation before us.

PAULINE KAEL: Movies indicate what the producers thought people would pay to see—which was not always the same as what they *would* pay to see. Even what they enjoyed seeing does not tell us directly what they believed but only indirectly hints at the tone and style of a culture. There is no reason to assume that people twenty or thirty years ago were stupider than they are now. (Consider how *we* may be judged by people twenty years from now looking at today's movies.) Though it may not seem obvious to us now, part of the original appeal of old movies—which we certainly understood and responded to as children—was that, despite their sentimental tone, they helped to form the liberalized modern consciousness. This trash—and most of it was, and is, trash—probably taught us more about the world, and even about values, than our "education" did. Movies broke down barriers of all kinds, opened up the world, helped to make us aware. And they were almost always on the side of the mistreated, the socially despised. Almost all drama is. And, because movies were a mass medium, they had to be on the side of the poor.[1]

MARSHALL MCLUHAN: In this respect the ad agencies function in relation to the commercial world much as Hollywood does in respect to the world of entertainment. In his cogent study, *The Hollywood Hallucination*, Parker Tyler summed it up in a sentence: "The movie theater is the psychoanalytic clinic of the average worker's daylight dream." That is, the spectator dreams in the darkened theater. He dreams the dreams that money can buy but which he can neither afford nor earn in the daylight world. In the dark theater he dreams the dreams which tend to keep even his frustrations within a dream world.

So Hollywood is like the ad agencies in constantly striving to enter and control the unconscious minds of a vast public, not in order to understand or to present these minds, as the serious novelist does, but in order to exploit them for profit. The novelist tries to get inside his characters in order to tell you what is happening on the invisible stage of their minds. The ad agencies and Hollywood, in their different ways, are always trying to get inside the public mind in order to impose their collective dreams on that inner stage. And in the pursuit of this goal both Hollywood and the advertising agencies themselves give major exhibitions of unconscious behavior.

[1] "Movies on Television" from **Kiss Kiss Bang Bang.** Copyright © 1965, 1966, 1967, 1968 by Pauline Kael. Originally appeared in *The New Yorker*, an Atlantic-Little, Brown title.

One dream opens into another until reality and fantasy are made interchangeable. The ad agencies flood the daytime world of conscious purpose and control with erotic imagery from the night world in order to drown, by suggestion, all sales resistance. Hollywood floods the night world with daytime imagery in which synthetic gods and goddesses (stars) appear to assume the roles of our wakeaday existence in order to flatter and console us for the failures of our daily lives.[2]

ALEXANDER WALKER: Nevertheless a moment's reflection shows that the dominant motif in the cinema has been sex appeal; and the stars chosen for study are those whose careers and lives off screen formed their characters in a way that assisted the peculiar kind of sex appeal associated with them on the screen. Some of them, of course, had this appeal deliberately created for them by others; and they then assimilated it into their performances and personalities. Often they regretted it: for the "image" stuck to them and resisted change. If there is any theme, apart from the sexual, that runs through ... it is the disorientating effect that stardom has on all but the most elemental wills.[3]

[2] "Love-Goddess Assembly Line." Reprinted by permission of the publisher, The Vanguard Press, from *The Mechanical Bride: Folklore of Industrial Man* by Marshall McLuhan. Copyright, 1951, by Herbert Marshall McLuhan.

[3] From *The Celluloid Sacrifice* by Alexander Walker.

the thirties: streamlined austerity and the glamorized no

Greta Garbo, serene and beautiful, but seeing into all, with futility at the end of everything. (Photo from the Bettman Archive, Inc.)

"Garbo reflected the malaise, the nervous discontent underlying the surface [of the era]. Through a combination of art, artifice, and accident, she began to capture the public imagination as a romantic, suffering recluse—a world-weary woman who went through the motions of living but who seemed always to foresee despair ahead."[4]

"I Can't Get Started"

I've flown around the world in a plane,
I've settled revolutions in Spain,
And the North Pole I have charted,
Still I can't get started with you.

On the golf course I'm under par,
Metro-Goldwyn have asked me to star,
I've got a house, a showplace,
Still I can't get no place with you.

I've been consulted by Franklin D.,
Greta Garbo has had me to tea,
But I'm broken hearted
'Cause I can't get started with you.[5]

The male voice singing this hit song is suave, sophisticated, and disillusioned. In "Grand Hotel" (1932) Garbo plays a similar type—a beautiful internationalite full of ennui. Why does the solitary, sad, oh-so-weary (but glamorous) world traveller stir the public's interest? Is this a 1930s version of the nineteenth century fascination with the Lord Byron figure and his own particular brand of *weltschmerz* (world-weariness)?

"'They don't have a type like me out here,' she wrote home in 1926, [Garbo to Sweden from Hollywood] and added a gloomy afterthought ... 'so if I can't learn to act they'll soon tire of me, I expect.' This was to be the tone all through her career. Success acted on Garbo like a depressant. By temperament she seems to have been pessimistic most of the time, which was a fruitful outlook when it could be incorporated into the tone of her films and make them very nearly plangent with fatalism."[6]

[4] Copyright © 1969 by Norman Zierold. From the book *Garbo.* Reprinted with permission of Stein and Day Publishers.
[5] "I Can't Get Started." Copyright © 1935 by Chappell & Co., Inc., copyright renewed. Used by permission of Chappell & Co., Inc.
[6] From *The Celluloid Sacrifice* by Alexander Walker.

> "The majority of Americans in the 1930s were not politically committed. They never marched on picket lines, protested against Wall Street, disclaimed 'counter-revolutionary formalism' and 'neo-Kantian banditism,' or took any interest in the Moscow Trials. For every citizen who had heard of the Communist Manifesto, read Lincoln Steffens's autobiography, sided with Stalinists or Trotskyists, or seen a production of the Group Theatre, there were thousands who had not. These people, of course, could not remain unaffected by the realities of scarcity and insecurity, but they could and did forget private problems by intermittently absorbing themselves in current fads, in spectator sports, in films and in vicariously living the lives of the great and notorious. Benny Goodman's swing jazz, the exploits of badman John Dillinger, the triumphs of the two great Joe's, Louis and DiMaggio, the cinematic dream world of Jean Harlow, Gary Cooper, and Clark Gable, ... compelled popular attention—not the internecine wars of the intelligentsia or the mare's nest of international politics.
>
> All the same, the wide-ranging consequences of the Depression affected directly or obliquely almost every phase of thought and activity during the Thirties: even the public diversions that helped to distract the masses from bread and butter concerns were not entirely uncolored by economic and political considerations. Anxieties tinged the popular jokes, crept into the popular songs. The strenuous efforts of press, radio, and film to evade Depression tensions almost had the effect of magnifying them, so discrepant from the real America beset by poverty, unemployment, and impending war was the picture of the joyful and prosperous America conjured up by the advertisers and scenario writers."[7]

It was at this time that the game Monopoly became a smashing success, employing fantasy-projections about property, business deals and, of course, money in a time when these were attainable by hardly anyone. Popular songs were "Headin' for Better Times," "I Found a Million Dollar Baby in a 5 & 10 Cent Store," and "We're in the Money" from "Gold Diggers of 1933" (one of a series of musicals in the 1930s about chorus girls hunting for rich men). Garbo, who went to work at 15 in Sweden to help support her family after her father's illness and death, constantly complained in America that she did not make enough money (often refusing to come to the studio—never actually arguing—until her salary was raised) and lived a relatively spartan life in Hollywood, investing her money wisely. She now lives well.

[7] From *The Strenuous Decade*, edited by Daniel Aaron and Robert Bendiner. Copyright © 1970 by Daniel Aaron and Robert Bendiner. Reprinted by permission of Doubleday & Company, Inc.

This conservatism, perhaps born of fatalism, became part of Garbo's public personality: " ... the screenplays of her [Garbo's] films, the very choice of stories, were designed to profit from the off-screen personality as it crystallised in the myth and the public's intense curiosity about her. The dour, melancholy, sexually enigmatic, neurotically shy Swede, who relaxed in men's clothes, viewed life fatalistically and talked like the archetypal Displaced Person of "going home"—these much advertised traits were worked into films which developed historical, erotic or romantic reasons for them, or else played the story dramatically in opposition to them."[8]

> "What would you say distinguished the Nineteen-Thirties from the 'post-war?'" For it is a very different time indeed ... What we are seeing is this. The world was getting, frankly, extremely silly ... it was getting into a really suffocating jam—no movement in any direction. A masquerade, a marking-time. Nothing real anywhere. It went on imitating itself with an almost religious absence of originality; and some of us foresaw an explosion. There must obviously arrive a point at which a breath of sense would break into it suddenly, and blow it all over. It's only a house of cards. Today [1937] we are in the process of being blown over flat."[9]
>
> "Aesthetics were out and politics were in, and sensibility was replaced by social awareness.... Martinis and champagne had given way to sherry and beer; serious-minded, aggressive pipes had ousted the gold-tipped Balkan Sobranie of yesteryear; Sulka shirts and Charvet ties were now outmoded by thick dark flannel and hairy tweed."[10]

The 1920s extravagance had become an impossibility, and a mood of seriousness prevailed. Is this why the American public empathized with the frugal Swede?

> "Garbo was something new for Hollywood. She was tall and broad-shouldered at a time when female stars were usually petite; pensive and reserved where the order of the day was flamboyance. The studio was in a quandary as to how to market her when suddenly the direction became clear. She was cast in her first film, **"The Torrent,"** and the response was electrifying.

[8] From *The Celluloid Sacrifice* by Alexander Walker.

[9] Wyndham Lewis, quoted in *Art Deco* by Bevis Hillier. Bevis Hillier: *Art Deco*, courtesy Studio Vista Publishers.

[10] Quote from *Art Deco*. Bevis Hillier: *Art Deco*, courtesy Studio Vista Publishers.

THE ONCE RICH[11]

Top to bottom:

Among Wall Street's four hundred neediest cases, the most pitiful is that of Bettina and Algernon. After expensively collected evidence, there's not a cent left for that Paris divorce.

The slump in the market is nothing compared to the slump in Mrs. Baggs' face when the doctor tells her that the third face-lift will cost her one hundred dollars an inch extra.

Conditions like this are deplorably prevalent among the newly-poor. Mrs. Wyllys has just fluttered in with the surprise: "Darling, we'll keep the cook, and I'll be your secretary."

No ostentatious thrift for Herbert, even if Albertina's money has gone to the bears. "If this is the best you can do," he announces, "I'm afraid our little Romance must end."

Le dernier cri in fashionable economy is doing one's own bootlegging. Decidedly chic this season, but Horace finds it a bit disconcerting under unsympathetic surveillance.

11 Anon, "The Once Rich." Courtesy *Harper's Bazaar* © Hearst Corporation 1931.

Audiences responded to a series of patterns which she was able to project. As a love object she combined the sensual with a spiritual appeal, femininity with a mannish quotient; she was as attractive to women as to men."[12]

This advertisement,[13] like the contemporaneous ad campaign featuring society ladies endorsing Camel cigarettes, stresses the femininity and acceptability of both a "mannish" look and the heretofore exclusively masculine act of smoking in public. Garbo went even farther by publicly rejecting traditional norms of heterosexual domesticity.[14]

[12] Copyright © 1969 by Norman Zierold. From the book *Garbo*. Reprinted with permission of Stein and Day Publishers.

[13] From the 1935 Sears, Roebuck and Co. catalog.

[14] Essay "Why I Will Not Marry" by Greta Garbo. Copyright 1932 Liberty Publishing Corp. Reprinted by permission of Liberty Library Corporation.

WHY I WILL NOT MARRY

GRETA GARBO

In Which the Celebrated Sphinx of the Screen Breaks Her Silence and Tells What Is in Her Heart

Why are people so interested in the matrimonial status of the film stars?

After all, marriage is "nobody's business" except the two people concerned. It is strictly their private affair.

Moreover, it is damaging to a star's following for the more intimate details of his or her domestic life to be broadcast far and wide. It is particularly unfair—if not actually unwise—in the case of the film actor who plays great-lover roles to stress the fact of his having a wife and children, no matter how he dotes on them in private.

Probably for this reason, if for no other, Hollywood no longer indulges in the big formal church weddings with gay banquets and dancing to follow—red-letter events like those which thrilled the film colony to the core when the nuptials of Vilma Banky and Rod La Rocque, Bebe Daniels and Ben Lyon were celebrated a few years ago.

Then, of course, there were the spectacular marriages of Gloria Swanson to her marquis, and of Mae Murray and Pola Negri to their brother princes Mdivani. Of these, Mae Murray's is the only marriage that has survived.

Despite the blaze of glory in which Gloria descended with the noble marquis upon Hollywood in 1925, and the fact that the film colony rose with one accord to do them honor, the romance was soon shattered. Not so soon, however, as that of Pola Negri. Last of the trio to wed, Pola was the first to shed her spouse. She beat Gloria to the divorce courts by just six days. Incidentally, both husbands have since found consolation elsewhere—Prince Serge (Pola's ex-husband) with the Chicago opera star Mary McCormick, while the Marquis de la Falaise de la Coudraye, *alias* "Hank," is now known as "Mr. Constance Bennett."

Personally, I should hate to have my husband lose his identity to that extent. Rather than that, I should want to retire from the screen altogether. I should want to forget I had ever been Greta Garbo.

With so many broken romances littered about the studios, Hollywood is not so keen as formerly to draw attention to the love affairs of its players.

Nowadays quiet weddings are the vogue.

It is the fashion to slip out of town by airplane, get married in far-away Mexico, and maybe or maybe not announce the fact afterward.

Ina Claire, reigning beauty of the New York stage, and John Gilbert, then prince of screen romantics, eloped by air to Las Vegas and were married there very quietly. Even so, bets were being made within two hours of the ceremony about the outcome of the marriage: that it wouldn't last a year; that it would survive six, eight, perhaps ten months.

What chance of success has the average marriage in these circumstances?

Can you wonder that film stars hesitate to exchange single blessedness for married bliss?

The particular problem that faces the film star, however, is this:

Have I the peculiar kind of genius and temperament that makes of matrimony a holy and lasting bond? Am I a fit and proper person to be anybody's "lawful wedded wife"? Can I make a success of married life?

With a male star, perhaps, it is different. When he marries, convention expects that his wife shall subordinate her interests to his, as happened recently in the case of Maurice Chevalier and Yvonne Vallée.

An artist in her own right, Yvonne relinquished her theatrical laurels gracefully, without complaint. When Maurice was invited to make pictures in Hollywood, it was as plain Mrs. Chevalier she urged him to accept, and as Mrs. Chevalier that she accompanied this internationally accepted exponent of charm.

How embarrassing, on the other hand, is the situation of the non-film-acting husband married to a famous film star! He is bound to lose something of his own identity. Imagine a man being known as "Mr. Garbo"—just that and nothing more!

And in those sections of society still impressed by the false glitter of the limelight, and where the spectacle of a woman who has made her own way in the world is still matter for surprise and idle chatter, this is what would surely happen.

Only a fool or a hero could abide such an anomalous position.

The only good reason for two people getting married is that they can be together most of the time. That is impossible with me so long as I remain on the screen.

The marriage contract which has to make the best of whatever is left over after the film contract has been fulfilled seems rather a makeshift affair. A husband needs his wife's thoughts and spiritual support as well as her actual physical presence. Unless one marries a fellow film artist, there is little chance of this ideal union of sympathy and interests. For I am in deadly earnest when I say that a film star's career is a whole-time job.

When I first went to Hollywood under the wing of the great Mauritz Stiller, I used to go to parties regularly and attend premières. But soon I found that my work began to suffer. Also, that to make public appearances destroys the illusion that surrounds the shadows of the silver sheet. The creative artist should be a rare and solitary spirit.

Stiller's death was a great blow to me. For so long I had been his satellite. All Europe at that time regarded Stiller as the most significant figure in the film world. Directors hurried to the projecting rooms where his prints were shown. They took with them their secretaries and, in the dim silence, they dictated breathless comments on the wide sweep of his magnificent technique.

Stiller had found me, an obscure artist in Sweden, and brought me to America. I worshipped him. There are some, of course, who say it was a love story. It was more. It was the utter devotion which only the very young can know—the adoration of a student for her teacher, of a timid girl for a master mind.

In his studio Stiller taught me how to do everything: how to eat; how to turn my head; how to express love—and hate.

Off the screen I studied his every whim, wish, and demand. I lived my life according to the plans he laid down. He told me what to say and what to do.

When Stiller died I found myself like a ship without a rudder. I was bewildered—lost—and very lonely. I resolutely refused to talk to reporters because I didn't know what to say.

By degrees I dropped out of the social whirl of Hollywood. I retired into my shell. I built a wall of repression around my real self, and I lived—and still live—behind it.

In the gayest, maddest colony in the world, I became a hermit.

I did not go to parties any more. I was too tired. I went to bed when my work at the studio was done.

If I needed recreation, I liked to be out of doors: to trudge about in a boy's coat and boy's shoes; to ride horseback, or shoot craps with the stable boys, or watch the sun set in a blaze of glory over the Pacific Ocean. You see, I am still a bit of a tomboy.

Most hostesses disapprove of this trousered attitude to life, so I do not inflict it upon them. Besides, I am still a little nervous, a little self-conscious about my English. I cannot express myself well at parties. I speak haltingly.

I feel awkward, shy, afraid.

In Hollywood, where every tea table bristles with gossip-writers, what I say might be misunderstood. So I am silent as the grave about my private affairs.

Rumors fly about. I am mum.

My private affairs are *strictly* private.

Does the demise of 1920s opulence, the concurrent emphasis on "reality," purposefulness, and frugality give rise to admiration for a movie star whose appeal is based on independence, self-denial, hard work—all the "masculine" virtues admired in "hard times" when one "goes it alone?" Garbo is reputed to have led a pristine life, working constantly and late at the studio, accompanied by various escorts but never strongly aligned with anyone (except perhaps her director-partner in work.) After working all day at the studio, she would, so her myth had it, return home for a solitary dinner in bed, and then go to sleep. When her one much-publicized–though apparently rather one-sided–"affair" with costar John Gilbert was over and someone mentioned his suicide attempts, her only comment was, "Oh, it's so silly." Was the adulation of a star who disparaged "nonsense" and lived monkishly predictable in an era that had been made to realize that seriousness and buckling down–not frippery–were the "wholesome" necessities of the day?

Many observers of Garbo's sexual appeal have noted that she can be very tender, passive and traditionally feminine, but that more often than not her strength and independent nature made her leading men appear dominated. "... imperceptibly, without conscious intention on anyone's part, she moved toward tragic roles as the Thirties wore on, and in tragedy lost her original masculine audience. It was hard to feel the dominant male with this superior woman whose eyes saw and discounted everything in advance."[15]

> "The way the spiritual and sexual natures are laminated together in Garbo's acting is what gives her scenes, especially her love scenes, their enigmatic character–this and her disturbing ability to change not only mood, but even gender, in the course of playing a part .... one feels Garbo really preferred screen lovers to be the passively romantic breed who rest *their* heads in *her* lap."[16]

Did this odd blend of spirituality and masculine-feminine sexuality produce the special quality that allowed the American public to view her often in the role of the sexual "vomp," (sic), as Garbo herself would say, yet think of her always as cold, detached, reserved, and certainly unsullied? Or was it that "the suffering of her soul was such that the American public would forgive all thirty-nine of her affairs in '**The Torrent**'?"[17]

Other individual attempts at frank and independent female sexuality in the period tend to appear scandalously risque and daring. Mae West is the obvious example.

[15] From *The Movies,* by Richard Griffiths and Arthur Mayer, © 1957, 1970 by Arthur Mayer and the estate of Richard Griffiths. Reprinted by permission of Simon and Schuster.

[16] From *The Celluloid Sacrifice* by Alexander Walker.

[17] From *The Celluloid Sacrifice* by Alexander Walker.

Cover, "George White's Scandals of 1936," permission by Chappell & Co., Inc.

Diana's DIARY

Some Bad News from Her Dream Man

Words and Picture by

BERT GREEN

(Reading time: 8 minutes 5 seconds.)

MONDAY: Oh gosh, all I do is read over David's telegram—"Tickled to death you have joined Scandals. I can't let my family know. Will explain later." I can't make out what he means by "Can't let my family know." First I thought they might object, then I thought it was just a phony excuse to cover up some other dame, but anyhow, I'm going to quit worrying till I hear from him.

Oh boy, this is the first day of my show girl career. Ever since I attached my curves to the fractured line in George White's Scandals the little kid has been all merried up, don't think she hasn't.

Who the hello would think that the Arcade Barber Shop's head manicurist would win a beauty prize an' be frolicking before the footlights? Manicuring may be alright Diary, but why should *I* be dipping guys' lunch hooks in finger bowls and be listening to a load of nitwit palava when I can just as well be cutting up steps and making merry to sin-co-pay-ted jazz? Listen Diary, if there's anything I crave, it's throwing a mean and hotsy hip to the bigger and better depression guys in the bald-headed row. Ab-so-lute-ly they love it! Yeah, and by the time "George" gets through putting me through the dance numbers, I'll be tossing a Rumba that will knock Havana's best hootch dancer for a row of empties, don't think I won't. This idea of being an actress has me tickled silly. Really, I just can't wait till the asbestos rises on the opening night so my great big "Dream Boy," David, can watch me step.

Shadylawn,
Southampton,
Long Island.

SWEETHEART,

When I got your sweet letter telling me that you had joined the Scandals, I was tickled pink. I think it's just grand.

Listen darling, I was so enthused I sprung it on the family, and my *mother went wild.*

She thinks that any girl that goes on the stage is headed for ruination. The poor dear is a bit old-fashioned in things like that.

To be very candid, she wants me to marry a society deb by the name of Gloria VanBexel, but to my way of thinking, there's nothing stirring! I'm so fed up with polo ponies, yachting parties, and social stuff, I'm all out of shape.

But don't you care Diana, I love you and that's all that matters. As soon as things blow over a little I'll be in to see you—perhaps early next week.

All my love,
DAVID.

Drawing and excerpt from "Diana's Diary." Copyright 1932 Liberty Publishing Corp. Reprinted by permission of Liberty Library Corporation.

DIANA'S DIARY

BERT GREEN

Some Bad News from Her Dream Man

Monday: Oh gosh, all I do is read over David's telegram—"Tickled to death you have joined Scandals. I can't let my family know. Will explain later." I can't make out what he means by "Can't let my family know." First I thought they might object, then I thought it was just a phony excuse to cover up some other dame, but anyhow, I'm going to quit worrying till I hear from him.

Oh boy, this is the first day of my show girl career. Ever since I attached my curves to the fractured line in George White's Scandals the little kid has been all merried up, don't think she hasn't.

Who the hello would think that the Arcade Barber Shop's head manicurist would win a beauty prize an' be frolicking before the footlights? Manicuring may be alright Diary, but why should I be dipping guys' lunch hooks in finger bowls and be listening to a load of nitwit palava when I can just as well be cutting up steps and making merry to sin-co-pay-ted jazz? Listen Diary, if there's anything I crave, it's throwing a mean and hotsy hip to the bigger and better depression guys in the bald-headed row. Ab-so-lute-ly they love it! Yeah, and by the time "George" gets through putting me through the dance numbers, I'll be tossing a Rumba that will knock Havana's best hootch dancer for a row of empties, don't think I won't. This idea of being an actress has me tickled silly. Really, I just can't wait till the asbestos rises on the opening night so my great big "Dream Boy" David, can watch me step.

Shadylawn,
Southampton,
Long Island.

SWEETHEART,

When I got your sweet letter telling me that you had joined the Scandals, I was tickled pink. I think it's just grand.

Listen darling, I was so enthused I sprung it on the family and my *mother went wild.*

She thinks that any girl that goes on the stage is headed for ruination. The poor dear is a bit old-fashioned in things like that.

To be very candid, she wants me to marry a society deb by the name of Gloria VanBexel, but to my way of thinking, there's nothing stirring! I'm so fed up with polo ponies, yachting parties, and social stuff, I'm all out of shape.

But don't you care Diana, I love *you* and that's all that matters. As soon as things blow over a little I'll be in to see you—perhaps early next week.

All my love,
DAVID.

The increasing independence of the female figure, of which Garbo was perhaps the first above-board example in film, was also happening in the arts.

> "Dogs were in favour, too, especially greyhounds and borzois, respectively suggested by the idea of streamlining and by the decorative dogs taken about by Hollywood stars. As the reposeful gave place to the dynamic, the Atalanta theme—a straining woman sprinter with flaring hair overtaking a greyhound—was enthusiastically rendered in virtually every material from Carrara marble to bronzed plaster and plastics ... The motifs of the thirties are more dynamic than the twenties: rising sun, racing clouds and hair streaming in the wind ... nudes gambolling under a blonde Aryan sun."[18]

Could Garbo's sexuality be acceptable to the American public because of the Nordic "purity" associated with her Scandinavian background?

[18] Quote from *Art Deco* by Bevis Hillier. Bevis Hillier: *Art Deco,* courtesy Studio Vista Publishers.

Cloud motif, from "God's Man" by Lynd Ward, 1930, from Art Deco. Bevis Hillier: Art Deco, courtesy Studio Vista Publishers.

Garbo photo, The Bettmann Archive (F 8242).

The most influential artistic movement of the 1930s, a school of design centered at the Bauhaus in Germany, made absolute values of clean streamlinedness, mass production, functionalism, high and direct lighting, glass and metal, and progress with a capital "P".

Collage of "The Modern Kitchen Is All Steel" and light fixtures from Sears catalog. From the 1935 Sears, Roebuck and Co. catalog.

RCA Building—Wendell MacRae, from Giedion's Space, Time and Architecture. Permission of Harvard University Press.

"Strictest economy must prevail in manufacturing buildings ... Therefore elimination of non-essentials and of everything not purely utilitarian is imperative. The very observance of this requirement, however, often makes for successful design. As a rule, the most direct and straightforward solution produces the best-looking structure. More buildings suffer from too much ornamentation than from too little. Just as the mere clothing of the skeleton of a modern airplane by designers with an eye for line and a sense of fitness produces an object of beauty, so the frank expression of the functional, the structural, element of the industrial building makes for success."[19]

Cover magazine Contempo. Reprinted from Art Deco. Bevis Hillier: Art Deco, courtesy Studio Vista Publishers.

The lighting used on Garbo was bright and harsh, emphasizing her thin, high-arched brows and her prominent bone structure, often with her hair pulled or brushed back from an exposed forehead. Coffee pots, vases, home artifacts of the 1930s are most often streamlined silver or smooth-curving metal with almost severely simple lines. Cigarette containers placed on coffee tables are low, sleek, simple and flat; even the cigarettes are sold in narrow packages called "flats." Geometric forms are popular, and purity of design is emphasized.

[19] "Architects on Defense" by Albert Kahn. Copyright © 1942 by The Atlantic Monthly Company, Boston, Mass. Reprinted with permission.

Greta Garbo photo. Used by permission of the Edward Steichen Collection.

A silver, horizontal, and stream-lined train.

How and why do silver, white, light, and metal come to represent "moderne" advancement for the 1930s? How do parallel structured and horizontal lines come to stand for progress? Why do Garbo's cameramen insist that her strong bones always show, using special white lighting to make them do so? (She dieted rigorously to make sure her bones were always "out.") Why are her cheekbones especially emphasized? Does Garbo come to represent some blend of the myths of American efficiency and European deeper knowledge?

Many claim that the adulation of Garbo was inspired by the peculiar ability of her face to mirror whatever her viewers were feeling. Her actual facial expression, said her director, changed not at all, only her eyes did. An actor said of her "Garbo is the hippie of the world, surveying the scene, never partaking of it, not even active enough to pass judgement. She becomes a mirror, and others finally see themselves in her... Garbo's quiet makes people see themselves in her, and finally they want to become like her."[20]

If Garbo is a "cool medium," in that she is a soft sell, not a frontal attack on the viewer's senses and sensibilities, how does this aid the 1930s audience in accepting her as both lady and sexual object? Her cult extended even to such things as a cartoon in the orthodox *Ladies Home Journal* where one of the "Tucker Twins" says to a barber, "Take some off in front, but I want it longer behind like Greta Garbo's." Seeing the elusive star in the flesh became a national obsession, "Thousands have drowned while lurking behind shrubbery in the hope of seeing her come out for a walk in the rain."[21]

[20] Quoted in *Garbo.* Copyright © 1969 by Norman Zierold. From the book *Garbo.* Reprinted with permission of Stein and Day Publishers.

[21] Quoted in *Garbo.* Copyright © 1969 by Norman Zierold. From the book *Garbo.* Reprinted with permission of Stein and Day Publishers.

Why is it that strong emotion in the package of low-keyed reticence and passivity so inspired the 1930s? What part does refusal to participate play in this? What warrants the sharp break between this and the frenetic activity of heroines in 1940s movies? Is wartime activity the only reason for the sudden shift?

1930s QUESTIONS AND PROJECTS

1. Find in your home or college town a building with a 1930s facade or interior. Write a building psychoanalysis showing how its design might manifest the mindset of the decade.

   Get some friends or drama students to go with you to a Salvation Army, Goodwill, or thrift store and find 1930s clothing. Write a scenario for and/or film a short episode reflecting the tone and concerns of the 1930s. Use the building for your set.

2. Design your own house or building, or furnish a room according to 1930s principles of design and decoration.

3. Prepare an advertisement for just about anything for an imaginary magazine or radio show, catering to a crossection of public interests in the 1930s. Make sure you keep prices, values, and popular materials and modes of construction in mind.

4. Look through magazines from around 1969 through 1972. What images, lines, materials and styles do you find that you would call "pure 30's?" For instance, slouch Garbo hats, finely arched eyebrows, sleek hairdos, crepe drapey dresses, bell-bottomed pants, and broad shoulders.

   What causes nostaliga for, and revival of, a certain era? Why was there so much attention given to the 1930s then? (Campy re-creations of 1930s musical revues—"**Dames at Sea**," "**The Boy Friend**," "**No, No, Nanette**.") Did the interest have anything to do with a similar economic condition? Or is nostalgia simply a cyclical pattern? (A few years ago Art Nouveau and fin de siecle—the 1890s—were all the rage.) The 1940s seem to be "in" at this date of publication: curly hair and red mouths, clunky platform shoes and tailored suits. Does this mean that soon everyone will be wearing bouffant hairdos, tiny-waisted cinch belts, and very full skirts as in the 1950s?

5. Find some sheet music and/or records, or look in the archives of your college library and copy down the words to popular songs of the 1930s. Write an analysis of the lyrics and try to determine the attitudes of the people they were created for.

6. Look at old movies on television and analyze the various star types, plots, and dominant motifs. Go to a film festival or to various showings of old films on your campus or elsewhere, and ask people why they are there, what they think of the film and how much of it they understand in relation to the era it was filmed in, and how they feel about the "old" stars and how much they know about them.

7. Ask your parents, grandparents, what "their" song was if they were courting in the 1930s. They will undoubtedly tell you how they felt about it and why.

8. Do you know, or know of, anyone whose charisma seems to result from what might be termed "positive refusal?" Find out about the romantic life of Queen Elizabeth I and see how it compares with Garbo's off and on screen life. (It was often suggested that she play this role.)

the forties: the exotic bad girl— pin-ups, mechanized sex, fun, and war

"Anybody who takes time to study the techniques of pictorial reportage in the popular press and magazines will easily find a dominant pattern composed of sex and technology. Hovering around this pair will usually be found images of hectic speed, mayhem, violence, and sudden death ...

To the mind of the modern girl, legs, like busts, are power points which she has been taught to tailor, but as parts of the success kit rather than erotically or sensuously. She swings her legs from the hip with masculine drive and confidence. She knows that 'a long-legged gal can go places.' As such, her legs are not intimately associated with her taste or with her unique self but are merely display objects like the grill work on a car. They are date-baited power levers for the management of the male audience."[22] (McLuhan, from essay by same title **The Mechanical Bride**).

"The trade motto 'Bodies by Fisher' is relevant to the present discussion because it insists on the close relation of motorcar glamour to sex, just as the feminine glamour ads and the modern beauty chorus insist on their relation to the machine.

These two ads help us to see one of the most peculiar features of our world—the interfusion of sex and technology. It is not a feature created by the ad men, but it seems rather to be born of a hungry curiosity to explore and enlarge the domain of sex by mechanical technique, on one hand, and, on the other, to *possess* machines in a sexually gratifying way."[23] (From "Love-Goddess Assembly Line" in **The Mechanical Bride**).

Never was the shotgun wedding of sex and technology so evident as during World War II. G.I.s, baffled and fascinated by a new war of elaborately powerful machines, were notorious (in a socially approved mode) for their psychosexual reliance on pin-ups of glamorous ladies. *Modern Screen* movie magazine ran a feature story about a young soldier dying in combat whose last words were "Goodbye, darling" to a bullet-pierced photo of Betty Grable.

Was this simply a natural phenomenon for American "boys away from home" in places like North Africa and the South Pacific, in the first major war in which mass-produced photographs from home were available? Or is

[22] "The Mechanical Bride." Reprinted by permission of the publisher, The Vanguard Press, from *The Mechanical Bride: Folklore of Industrial Man* by Marshall McLuhan. Copyright, 1951, by Herbert Marshall McLuhan.

[23] "Love-Goddess Assembly Line." Reprinted by permission of the publisher, The Vanguard Press, from *The Mechanical Bride: Folklore of Industrial Man* by Marshall McLuhan. Copyright, 1951, by Herbert Marshall McLuhan.

there something more sinister, as McLuhan believes, in those highly stylized photos that, if they do not mechanize sex, still successfully reinforce the separation of the pinup admirer from actual human contact? Also allegedly "humanizing" the harsh daily reality of war is another surrogate: the sexlessly pure, idealized "girl back home." Much less revealingly seductive in her photos than the sex queen, she perhaps salves the Puritan conscience. But both extremes are equally idealized and unreal.

"I've Been Drafted Now I'm Drafting You"

I want someone to cry when I'm away,
I want someone to write me every day;
Someone sweet and lovable, somebody true,
I've BEEN DRAFTED, (Now I'm Drafting You)

I want somebody's picture in my tent,
I want someone to cheer my regiment:
Someone who'll be thrilled when I march in review.
I'VE BEEN DRAFTED (now I'm Drafting You)

My Country called me to do my part,
My Country needs me and I need you, sweetheart
I want someone who's heart will volunteer
To wait for me at least another year,
Someone there with open arms, when camp is thru.
I'VE BEEN DRAFTED, (now I'm Drafting You).[24]

Rita Hayworth, famous for her femme-fatale movie roles, was a most popular G.I. pinup. On film, she appears imminently accessible, but, in the classic guise of the tease, really just moves *through.* She may be tantalizingly close, but predictably the fantasies surrounding her can never become realizable, and so are never disappointed. Elusiveness may be an inherent part of the man-killer image.

[24] Copyright 1941. Vanguard Songs. Used by special permission.

Cover of sheet music "Sadie Thompson's Song (The Blue Pacific Blues)," from Columbia Pictures' "Miss Sadie Thompson" © 1953 by Mills Music Inc. Lyrics by Ned Washington, music by Lester Lee. Permission granted by Belwin Mills Publishing Corp.

In this scene from "**Gilda**," Rita Hayworth dances through a crowd of people in a casino in far-away Buenos Aires. They reach out, unsuccessfully, to touch her as she strips off her gloves suggestively and sings *"Put the Blame on Mame, Boys."* Would it be pushing the connection too far to say that depersonalized unrealized sexuality, constantly stimulated, provokes the kind of schizophrenic divorce from human reality that makes men able to become killing machines?

The bomb dropped on Hiroshima was named "Gilda."

From the Bettmann Archive, Inc.,
from "Gilda."

> "Our plane, which Marlow had nicknamed *The Body*, was one of those aircraft that announce, on the first day's flight, that they are all right, in every response and utterance they are like a Lincoln Continental or a perfect pussy cat ... He handled all that airplane with his finger tips, and his movements were gradual, and the ship's were smooth ... He held the wheel the way he'd hold a martini glass and a butt when he thought he was snowing a dame ... A few minutes later, though, as we walked around the plane he seemed to think of the ship as a *her*, and he came close to giving her the name she eventually carried. 'Some torso, huh?' he said. 'Just seeing that thing makes me feel horny. I can't wait to get my hands on her.' "[25] (from **The War Lover**)

Not only does Hayworth emerge in the long run as unpossessable, but she is also nearly always placed in a far-away setting, cast as a type foreign or, at least, hardly all-American. As an outsider or exile, she attains a trapped, pent-up quality that seems to add to her animal vitality and seductiveness.

"The Blue Pacific Blues"

I'm gettin' The Blue Pacific Blues,
The feelin' you get from real bad news.
I wanna hear bells, I wanna see trains,
I get in this mood whenever it rains:
I'm gettin' the Blues!

Alone in the dark and sultry night,
You think of the times you ain't done right
To add to the fact you're feelin' so bad,
The cry of the birds keeps drivin' you mad:
It's part of the Blues!

You lie awake, and how you wish that it was morning!
And then you smoke a hundred cigarettes or more.
That devil Rain, continues poundin' on your window
And the Tropic winds keep howlin' at your door.

Regardless of all the rain and mud,
The feel of the place gets in your blood.
But deep in the night there comes unawares
The terrible thought that nobody cares:
You're back with the Blues again.[26]

[25] From *The War Lover* by John Hersey, 1959, Alfred A. Knopf, Inc.

[26] Lyrics to *"The Blue Pacific Blues"* © 1953 by Mills Music Inc. Lyrics by Ned Washington, music by Lester Lee. Permission granted by Belwin Mills Publishing Corp.

Photo of Hayworth from The Movies. Used by permission of Arthur L. Mayer, as a reprint from The Movies © 1957, 1970 by Arthur Mayer and the Estate of Richard Griffiths. Reprinted by permission of Simon and Schuster.

Central photo from sheet music cover of "Sadie Thompson's Song (The Blue Pacific Blues)" from Columbia Pictures' "Miss Sadie Thompson" © 1953 by Mills Music Inc. Lyrics by Ned Washington, music by Lester Lee. Permission granted by Belwin Mills Publishing Corp.

Hayworth seems at first to be a familiar type; the glamorous vamp—Clara Bow, Theda Bara, Jean Harlow, Elizabeth Taylor—the "Bad Girl" of the movie screen who is allowed to do things in and out of the movies that the "real" American "Good Girl" would never be allowed to do.

> "In '**God Is My Co-Pilot**,' the G.I.'s agreed that what they were fighting for was, after all, the American girl ... No matter how much thigh she may be demurely sporting, she is sweet, nonsexual, and immaturely innocent ... Coke ads concentrate on the 'good girl' image as opposed to the dominant 'bad girl' of popular entertainment ... The present coke ad [1951] features a Laura Dearborn, an old-fashioned mother-cum-sweetheart type, a dream drinking. This is the type portrayed in Ingrid Bergman. Recently the furor over her Rossellini affair was an interesting example of what happens when two dreams get crossed up. She wantonly stepped out of her Hollywood stereotype, endangering a large investment. Rita Hayworth's stereotype, on the other hand, was not shattered by her affair."[27]

The glamour of the elusive "man-killer" remains fascinating even when she is reprehensible, and maybe even *because* she is.

"Tangerine"

Tangerine, she is all they claim
With her eyes of fire
And lips as red as flame.

Tangerine, when she dances by,
Senoritas stare,
And caballeros sigh.

And I've seen, clothes on Tangerine
Where the label says from Macy's mezzanine
Yes she's got the boys in a whirl
But she's only fooling one girl
She's only fooling Tangerine.[28]

[27] "Cokes and Cheesecake." Reprinted by permission of the publisher, The Vanguard Press, from *The Mechanical Bride: Folklore of Industrial Man* by Marshall McLuhan. Copyright, 1951, by Herbert Marshall McLuhan.

[28] *"Tangerine"* by Famous Music Corporation 1942, © renewed by Famous Music Corporation 1969.

War conditions in Europe made it necessary to glamorize (and to capitalize on) Mexico and South America. This resulted in the promotion of Carmen Miranda types, wearing great floppy fruit hats in extravagant and clichéd dance numbers. A consequent subcraze populated American middle-class households with innumerable plaster shuffling donkeys, sombreroed sleepers and, indeed, the Chiquita Banana logo, costumed and dancing as though she were Carmen Miranda herself.

Rita Hayworth's exotic allure was amplified by her actual history as a Mexican dancer. A family member of the Cansino dance troupe, Hayworth, although glamorized by Columbia Studios, never lost her "primitive" appeal. In the Orient, South America, and Spain, she sings and dances with smooth seductiveness or gypsy-like abandon (**"The Lady from Shanghai," "Gilda," "Blood and Sand," "The Loves of Carmen"**).

"Blood and Sand," Culver Pictures.

Popular movie songs in the 1940s often had gypsy/Latin motifs: *"In a Little Spanish Town," "In Acapulco," "Golden Earrings" ("A gypsy told me . . .), "A Rainy Night in Rio," "Amado Mio"* (from "**Gilda**"), or else impossibly romantic and colorful, often tropical, auras: *"The Last Time I Saw Paris," "Blue Shadows and White Gardenias," "Blue Tahitian Mood."*

From the 1945 Sears, Roebuck and Co. catalog.

Movies abounded with the title "**Road to . . .** "–**Morocco, Rio, Bali, Tahiti, Utopia**–nearly every place that could be filled with "natives" and ridiculously romanticized.

Was it easier for the American movie audience to accept seductiveness and abandon from a type quite clearly *not* all-American? Is a Latin or dark, female figure sometimes a more acceptable screen vehicle for the American enjoyment of sex? What significance is there to the notion that sexual intrigue and mystery go on more frequently elsewhere, in situations not ever realizable by the average movie goer? "**Casablanca**" comes most immediately to mind. And look what happens to Woody Allen in "**Play It Again, Sam.**"

Airplanes were advertised as BIG BIRDS ready to take you anywhere glamorous.

"You Belong To Me"

See the pyramids along the Nile,
Watch the sunrise on a tropic isle,
Just remember darling, all the while—
You belong to me.

See the marketplace in old Algiers,
Send me photographs and souvenirs,
Just remember when a dream appears,
You belong to me.

I'll be so alone without you,
Maybe you'll be lonesome too, and blue.

Fly the ocean in a silver plane,
See the jungle when it's wet with rain,
Just remember till you're home again,
You belong to me.[29]

Compare this songs' lyrics to, for example, *"Button Up Your Overcoat,"* from the 1930s:

Button up your overcoat
When the wind blows free
Take good care of yourself
You belong to me.

Eat an apple every day
Get to bed by three
Take good care of yourself
You belong to me.

Be careful crossing streets (oo-oo)
Don't eat meats (oo-oo)
Cut out sweets (oo-oo)
You'll get a pain and hurt your tumtum.

Stay away from bootleg booze
When you're on a spree
Take good care of yourself
You belong to me.[30]

Is there not only a strong emphasis in *"You Belong to Me"* on the glamorization of "foreign" lands but also a sharply different attitude about the fear of outside experience? How might this reflect a shift from a time of necessarily tight economic structure to a decade when international travel has been made more familiar by wartime movement, and the economy is more secure, more lavish? Are people just less afraid of everything when they have more money?

[29] From *"You Belong to Me"* with permission of The Big 3 Music Company.
[30] *"Button Up Your Overcoat."* Copyright © 1928 by DeSylva, Brown & Henderson, Inc. Copyright renewed—assigned to Chappell & Co., Inc. Used by permission of Chappel & Co., Inc.

"War, like crime, may not pay, but it certainly helps the boxoffice. By 1942 everybody not in the army was working, making more money than ever before, and looking for an agreeable way to spend it. What with gas rationing, the automobile was worthless for speeding to roadhouses or necking on lonely lanes. Night baseball was out for the duration. TV was as yet only a faint disturbance on the distant air waves. Few new homes were available, and there were no refrigerators or washing machines to make the few that were available homelike. So that, though the bright lights of the theater marquees were browned out on Broadway and Main Street, the absence of illumination did not diminish the public's appetite for what was inside the theaters. Exhibitors gaily quipped, 'You can open a can of sardines and there's a line waiting to get in.' "[31] (from **The Movies**)

The craving for entertainment extended to other areas, too, with lavishness and opulence the general keynote: (From *Life's* article "Earl Carroll's", February 14, 1944:)

"Few night clubs in the world are as big or as ornate as the Hollywood theater-restaurant owned by Earl Carroll, whose dunking of an unclad showgirl in a bathtub of champagne once made him considerable trouble. Like Hollywood's other huge hotspot, the Florentine Gardens (*Life*, January 31), Carroll's favors a sexy approach in its entertainment. Both places emphasize the beauty of the partially-draped female form; both feature games in which customers have an opportunity to make themselves appear silly. At the Gardens the girls do the hula with servicemen; at Carroll's, servicemen play a game in which they try to lace the showgirls' corsets while the girls wiggle. But where the barnlike Gardens smacks of the honky-tonk, Carroll's seems almost artistic. The difference lies in Carroll's showmanship. He realized now, as he did when he used to produce his Vanities, that it is possible to lend an aura of respectability to the flesh and the devil by presenting them in gorgeous costumes against a sumptuous background."[32]

Like Playboy Bunnies, the showgirls only "fraternize" with the customers as a part of the show, which is of course packaged and only obtainable by money.

[31] Used by permission of Arthur L. Mayer, as reprinted from *The Movies.* © 1957, 1970 by Arthur Mayer and the estate of Richard Griffiths. Reprinted by permission of Simon and Schuster.

[32] Excerpt from *Life's* February 14, 1944 article "Earl Carroll's." Copyright *Life* magazine.

"Circular staircase" is one of V for Venus' *most spectacular numbers. Girls slowly descend the staircase, walk out among the closely packed audience and then return to the stage. From Life's February 14, 1944 article "Earl Carroll's." Copyright Life magazine.*

"More night clubs were making more money than ever before. On Feb. 3 pari-mutuel betting at Hialeah topped $1,000,000 for the first time in the history of Florida. Hotels, booked solidly through March, were turning away dozens of would-be patrons each day.

This reversion to prewar indulgence contrasts sharply with the continued diligence of servicemen, war-plant workers, and others whom war has brought to Miami ... it was as though someone had called off the war. Upon these hotels, upon every boardinghouse and cottage in the city, hordes of hedonists, defying the Government's request not to travel for fun, descended from the north by train, by bus and in private cars propelled by black-market gasoline.

... A track employee at Hialeah observed last week: 'We're having some fun this winter for a change.' "[33]

"Leg show attracts crowds to Sea Pool Sun and Cabana Club. Disabled war veterans (in front rows) were special guests; others paid $1.10 admission. War bonds were awarded to exhibitors of best legs."[34]

[33] Excerpt from *Life's* February 21, 1944 "Miami Spectacle." Copyright *Life* magazine.
[34] From *Life's* February 21, 1944 "Miami Spectacle." Rights held by photographer Jerry Cooke of 161 E. 82nd Street, New York, N. Y.

Is this fun-seeking flamboyance a reaction to 1930s deprivation? The natural product of a booming wartime economy? Or some new edge of increasing American technopleasure hysteria? How does having a good time begin to be defined in terms of the concrete acquisition, grandiose display, and overwhelming consumption of opulently tangible material stuff?

The technologizing of big-scale fun includes the technologizing of sex. And the framing and mechanization of some women as spectacular sex-objects is paralleled, interestingly, by the worship of the All-American Girl, who represents the secure all-American material well being of "life in the States."

> "We were ready to die to the last man for Dinah Shore, rare sirloin, a cold beer, and a Caribbean cruise. Maybe we didn't put much stock in the Four Freedoms; that was propaganda. But we really believed in *Time* and the *Post* and *Colliers* and *Life.*"[35]
>
> A wartime ad shows a soldier fighting far away, dreaming of home: "Out here, I hope . . . Out here, I think . . . Out here, I dream of peace—and coming home to showers and clean sheets and Christmas trees and apple pies and my job . . . and the girl I love. I *will* come home again . . . "

The high stylization and glamorization of costume here extends even to the shoes; while the whole outfit is impossibly lavish and unreal, the attitude is definitely come hither. What, for instance, might one make of the calculated open-toe shoes, typically 1940s, which are invitingly fleshy yet highly structured. What does the juxtaposition of metallic glitter and bare flesh suggest?

The extravagance and unreality in combination with a definite seductiveness can lead to a desire-frustration stalemate.

[35] *The War Lover* by John Hersey, 1959, Alfred Knopf, Inc.

"Ravishing Rita," The Bettmann Archive.

1944 Firestone Ad.

The desire for fun, goods, universal *fullness*, seems to result in a cornucopia motif of overflowing merchandise and bosoms.

Shapes are rotund or jam-packed; largeness is a virtue. People dance "The Big Apple," and buy (or at least want to buy) cars that look like this:

1947 Cadillac. Cadillac Motor Division, M & E Photographic.

And furniture was comfortably rounded:

From the 1945 Sears, Roebuck and Co. catalog.

In nearly every advertisement and on every glamorous lady, mouths are bright red, moist, curved and full; Joan Crawford's becomes her trademark, the "mouth that won't quit." Colored nails most often match lips, and the combination, on these "essences of femininity," is violent, a disturbingly blood-dipped quality. Evening gowns, unlike the sleek, flowing satin lines of the 1930s, are bedecked with sequins, feathers, ruffles, and even ermine tails.

Bodies are never angular. "Going all out" becomes an ideal; songs like *"ac-Cent-Tchuate the Positive"* advise people to forget *"The Negative"* and *"watch out for Mr. In-Between."* Bands are Big, and so is "swinging out." Everyone rushes to get the first "new," postwar automobiles, refrigerators, and stoves.

And Rita Hayworth marries the richest prince (and a glamorous Persian potentate at that) in the world.

Photo of Rita Hayworth and Aly Kahn. UPI.

1940s QUESTIONS AND PROJECTS

1. Make a collection of slang terms describing sexual situations and processes that are drawn from mechanical jargon. "Screw" is one example; others will certainly suggest themselves. List mechanical, technical, and particularly military terms used to describe women and female behavior such as "A blonde bomb." What, on the other hand, are some feminine qualities attributed (in the vernacular) to cars, planes, and weapons?

   Think about the literal meaning of these terms in the reversed context. What does this transference imply to you about the innate evaluation of people and relationships?

   Consult a slang dictionary and chronologically correlate the phrases you have gathered by the dates of origin given.

2. Find periodicals of the decade and examine the short popular fiction of the adventure-romantic genre, or go to your local newspaper and use their archives to survey cartoon strips of the 1940s. Catalogue the female types that appear and organize them on a scale from the most "evil" to the most "pure." Where does the "Dragon Lady" go? "Blondie?" Re-rate the characters as "exotic" or "corn-fed."

   Can you find any pattern, geographic or socioeconomic, in how close to or far away from the middle-American "home" the various types are usually found? Correlate this with the degree of sexual allure. Who's in Hong Kong? Who's in the kitchen?

   Why would someone not expect to, or not want to, be allured at home? Who would that someone be?

3. Dig around in old trunks for pinups of movie stars and glamour girls. Try to determine which particular female body shapes and emotional moods are emphasized. Examine advertisements in old issues of *Life, Look,* and the like. Can you make a comparison between the shapes of the pinups and the merchandise? Between the mood of the picture and the tone of the ad?

   Select a sampling of ads for "luxury" merchandise. How many have women in them? What kind of women? How many have men? How many of the men are soldiers? How many of the soldiers are with which kinds of women? What are the soldiers and women doing, thinking, and feeling? What does it have to do with the merchandise? Which really *is* the merchandise?

4. While you have these 1940s ads at hand, lay them out with some from the 1930s. Try some thematic comparison and contrast speculations. Look, for instance, at the mouths of the ladies. What is going on?

5. Watch American war movies on TV and try to determine the stock myths of G.I. attitudes about sex and women. What are the standard modes of feeling about and relating to the girl-back-home expressed by the Hollywood "dogface?" And his feelings for and relations with the girls native to the country in which he's stationed?

   Watch "**The Man in the Gray Flannel Suit**," if you can, and then find World War II veterans willing to reminisce about their romantic adventures overseas. Then ask them about their first date back home. Try uncles and neighbors; your father or grandfather probably wouldn't tell the truth anyway.

6. See the movie "**M*A*S*H**"; read or watch "**Catch-22**". Review Lieutenant Calley's explanation of the events at My Lai. What do you think of the idea of a separation between who you are, or what you believe in, and what you do? How does this separation occur? Does technology necessarily play a part in such a division?

   Does this phenomenon lend itself readily to sexual experience? To sexual fantasy? If so, why and how?

   If you believe there is some kind of interrelation, how would you diagram the interworkings among the input of self, mechanization, the media, war, sex, and the output of production, victory, and love. Can love be victory? Can victory be successful production? How does the removal of the real self, or of the self from reality, encourage this confusion? What happens to the self in the process?

7. Have the G.I.'s of the 1970s in Asia focused on any heroine or sex goddess to come home to? Interview some returned veterans and find out if they had any ideal of the American girl or representative of the American way of life in mind while they were in action. If there is an ambiguity about universally admired symbols, does this have to do with a general ambiguity about the whole present war effort? Or does it have to do with a special quality of the 1960s and 1970s? How? Why?

   If mechanization in love or war serves to protect the self by creating an isolating distance, what happens when the machine works too well and ends up forcing the self into intimate contact with what the self is doing? How would a 1940s G.I. feel in a contemporary Asian street situation where "anybody could be an enemy"? In "civvies," how would he feel in a contemporary American street situation where, in lieu of exotically painted women, "any chick would be a 'number' "? What do numbers (body-counts) have to do with death? and what do they have to do with sex?

8. If there were to be a revival of the 1950s, as there has been of the 1930s

and 1940s, try to visualize the revival in terms of clothing, art, furniture, and music. The periods we are nostalgic about seem to be closer and closer to the current age—in World War II America was nostalgic about the Civil War, and "**Gone with the Wind**," for example, in the early 1960s about the 1890s, and in the late 1960s and early 1970s about the 1930s and 1940s. Is this America in a hurry even to "look back"? What will happen if we catch up with ourselves?

9. In Scene 6 of "**The Glass Menagerie**," Tom says, "All of those glamorous people—having adventures—hogging it all, gobbling the whole thing up! You know what happens? People go to the *movies* instead of *moving*! Hollywood characters are supposed to have all the adventures for everybody in America while everybody in America sits in a dark room and watches them have them.! Yes, until there's a war. That's when adventure becomes available to the masses! *Everyone's* dish, not only Gable's! Then the people in the dark room come out of the dark room to have some adventures themselves—goody, goody! It's our turn now, to go to the South Sea Island—to make a safari—to be exotic, far-off!" Does this partially explain why "ordinary" people do extraordinary, unreal things during wars? If you've been trained to think that it is all an adventure in a specially designed set (that you may have seen before on the screen) it might be easy to remove yourself from the possible consequences of your actions, to truly become a Superstar.

the fifties: bringing it all home with the innocent-blonde, synthetically natural sex queen

Marilyn in "The Seven Year Itch." (The Bettmann Archive, Inc.)

The big thing about Marilyn Monroe was always her spontaneity and her essential innocence. This was why, people said, her movies never, (well almost never) made *SEX* seem dirty or undignified. It wasn't sultry or enigmatic. It was just right out there, and, despite all the analysis about what it was that made her different from, for instance, Jayne Mansfield or Carroll Baker, well, in the end all you could say was that she and her femaleness were just there better than with any other star. So America forgave her the nude calendar, the shady background, the different marriages. She, a sex queen, even sang *Happy Birthday* to President John F. Kennedy in Madison Square Garden.

For she gave America what it needed at the time—bounce, and real sex, and plenty of it, with no bones about it (no pun) and she managed always to give the impression that she just hardly knew what was going on. So who could blame her? You weren't being taken in, or seduced, or used, or made to feel as if you had gone to a "skin" movie that you couldn't tell your wife about (you might even take the whole family) because it was certain that THAT intent wasn't there on her part. And it was probably all in good fun.

In the movie "**The Seven Year Itch**," Monroe manages to visit her downstairs neighbor every evening during a very hot summer. He is a restlessly married man left alone while his wife is on vacation. Monroe does things like putting her underpants in his refrigerator to cool them off, bringing champagne, making *double entendres* about the heat and so on, and the whole time she ingenuously appears as if she were a little girl away at summer camp for the first time. Monroe says, "I think that sexuality is only attractive when it's natural and spontaneous ... I never quite understood it—this sex symbol—I always thought symbols were those things you clash together. That's the trouble, a sex symbol becomes a thing. But if I'm going to be a symbol of something I'd rather have it sex than some other things they've got symbols of!"[36]

LITTLE GIRL ALIAS FEMME FATALE[37]

CECIL BEATON

Miss Marilyn Monroe calls to mind the bouquet of a fireworks display, eliciting from her awed spectators an openmouthed chorus of wondrous ohs and ahs. She is as spectacular as the silvery shower of a Vesuvius fountain;

[36] "Marilyn Lets Her Hair Down," by Richard Meryman. *Life,* August 3, 1962, © 1962 Time Inc.

[37] "Little Girl Alias Femme Fatale" by Cecil Beaton. Courtesy Cecil Beaton/*Harper's Bazaar.*

she has rocketed from obscurity to become our postwar sex-symbol—the pin-up girl of an age. And whatever press agentry or manufactured illusion may have lit the fuse, it is her own weird genius that has sustained her flight.

Transfigured by the garish marvel of Technicolor and Cinemascope, she walks like an undulating basilisk, scorching everything in her path but the rosemary bushes. Her voice has the sensuality of silk or velvet.

But the real marvel lies in the paradox—somehow we know that this extraordinary performance is pure charade, a little girl's caricature of Mae West. The puzzling truth is that Miss Monroe is a make-believe siren, unsophisticated as a Rhine maiden, innocent as a sleep-walker. She is an urchin pretending to be grown up, having the time of her life in mother's moth-eaten finery, tottering about in high-heeled shoes and sipping ginger ale as though it were a champagne cocktail. There is an unwordly, a winsome naiveté about the child's eyes that, quick as a flash, will screw up into a pair of sexy, smoldering slits and give you a synthetic "come-hither" look. Just as obligingly, the delicate, flexible mouth, half-parted in springtime ecstasy, will burst into a generous grimace, displaying flawless seed-pearl teeth while the surrounding lips quiver nervously and seem almost shocking in their mobile suggestiveness.

Behind this brilliant, pseudo-fatal facade is the real Marilyn Monroe. She might be the latter-day incarnation of a Greuze portrait, the quintessence of partridge-plump prettiness with full, high breasts, eighteenth-century rump and a delicately modeled face—eyes felicitously wide apart, chin appealingly small, putty-like nose created expressly for wrinkling up with delight, or for photography (though in profile the urchin is apt to gain the ascendancy).

Passing across these enviable features, like blips on a radar screen, is an incredible display of inspired, narcissistic moods. With the possible exception of a Scotch landscape, there has seldom been such an everchanging subject for the photographer. He may miss recording one mood, but a dozen others will assault him with machine-gun recompense.

In her presence, you are startled, then disarmed, by her lack of inhibition. What might at first seem like exhibitionism is yet counter-balanced by a wistful incertitude beneath the surface. If this star is an abandoned sprite, she touchingly looks to her audience for approval. She is strikingly like an over-excited child asked downstairs after tea. The initial shyness over, excitement has now gotten the better of her. She romps, she squeals with delight, she leaps onto the sofa. She puts a flower stem in her mouth, puffing on a daisy as though it were a cigarette. It is an artless, impromptu, high-spirited, infectiously gay performance. It may end in tears.

Equally impromptu is her general appearance. This canary blond nymph has been so sufficiently endowed by nature as to pay no attention to the way she looks. Her hair, her nails, her make-up, have a makeshift, spontaneous attractiveness. It is all very contemporary: Marilyn Monroe conjures up two straws in a single soda, juke boxes, sheer nylons and drive-in movies for necking (does she not project a hypnotized nymphomania?).

This, then, is the wonder of the age—a dreaming somnambule, a composite of Alice in Wonderland, Trilby and a Minsky artist. Perhaps she was born the postwar day we had need of her. Certainly she has no knowledge of the past. Like Giradoux' Ondine, she is only fifteen years old; and she will never die.

The 1950s, many people now feel, was primarily a decade of psychological whitewash. Innocence and placidity (real or pretended) covered over a mass of social and political turbulence that would later burst forth in 1960s disillusionment, uprisings, recriminations.[38] But for the time being, an attitude of ignorance was preferred; even if each person knew of wild beach parties and goings-on in convertible back seats, these things were kept *sotto voce*, for the official image, anyway—young people lived theoretically as the youngsters did in the Archie comic books: meeting after school over checked gingham table cloths at Pop's corner drugstore soda fountain to see the rest of the gang.

Is it any wonder, then, that the American public chose for its sex symbol this cheery, naive, apparently dumb blonde? And if strong censorship and traditionally acceptable plots were gradually replaced by a loosening of restrictions and more "realistic" movies, so, interestingly, did Monroe's roles change. From the stock blonde comedy figure in the early films ("**How to Marry a Millionaire**") she would progress to sophisticated comedy like "**Some Like it Hot**," in which she charitably attempts to seduce a theoretically impotent Tony Curtis (he isn't really) with complex and comic results. The progression even extended to drama, as in the realistic "**The Misfits**," where she is a sexually over-mature woman who's been around a bit too much or too long. Similarly, song lyrics from early 1950s movies featured romanticized girls and places. There was a gradual change in song titles, from "**Girl Upstairs**" in "**The Seven Year Itch**," to "**Something's Gotta Give**," with implications soon becoming

[38] Read Michael Harrington's *The Other America* for the first documentation of the new awareness that all was not well with the affluent America of the Eisenhower years. And also read *The 1950's—America's "Placid Decade,"* edited by Joseph Satin, for a discussion of conformity and "cheerful robotry."

more and more unavoidable: "**The Girl Can't Help It**," "**Untamed Youth**," "**The Opposite Sex**," "**An Affair to Remember**." Whether Monroe triggered the change to a greater openness, or whether she simply reflected it, America seems to have accepted her increasing sexuality because she was originally and consistently ingenuous, blonde, and endearing.

After deciding to "make it in the movies," and after a long struggling period of waiting—and even scrimping for food—Marilyn is shaped up by her agent: "Back in Los Angeles with her decree [divorce from an early marriage] Norma Jean [Monroe's real name] found Emmeline full of plans. She privately believed her protegée's hair needed altering. It wasn't really blonde enough. It was also kept so tightly curled by permanents that on one occasion when a pillbox hat was placed on her head, the effect was comical. 'I have a call for a light blonde, honey or platinum. Wavy, not curly hair,' Emmeline told her.

The change was accomplished in one session at the beauty salon, and the shampoo client had helped create a new and more negotiable Norma Jean."[39]

The admiration for things blonde in the 1950s extended even to very light-colored furniture, known as blonde wood.

When Monroe was working in "**Gentlemen Prefer Blondes**" with brunette Jane Russell, she could not obtain a private dressing room. Later, Monroe said of that experience, "Jane Russell—she was the brunette in it and I was the blonde—she got $200,000 for it and I got my $500 a week, but that to me was, you know, considerable. She, by the way, was quite wonderful to me. The only thing was I couldn't get a dressing room. I said, finally—I really got to this kind of level—I said, "look, after all, I am the blonde and it is "**Gentlemen Prefer Blondes**!" Because still they always kept saying, "Remember, you're not a star," I said, 'Well, whatever I am, I *am* the blonde!' "[40]

Was America simply a country with Nordic, Teutonic prejudices and preferences in the 1950s, as always? (The blonde being essentially the good, innocent, all-American girl.) What might one make then of the generally accepted notion that blondes *could* and *did* have "more fun" (that is, sexual license)

[39] From *Norma Jean* by Fred Lawrence Guiles. Copyright 1969 by Fred Lawrence Guiles. Used with permission of McGraw-Hill Book Company.

[40] From "Marilyn Lets Her Hair Down" by Richard Meryman, *Life*, August 3, 1962, © 1962 Time Inc.

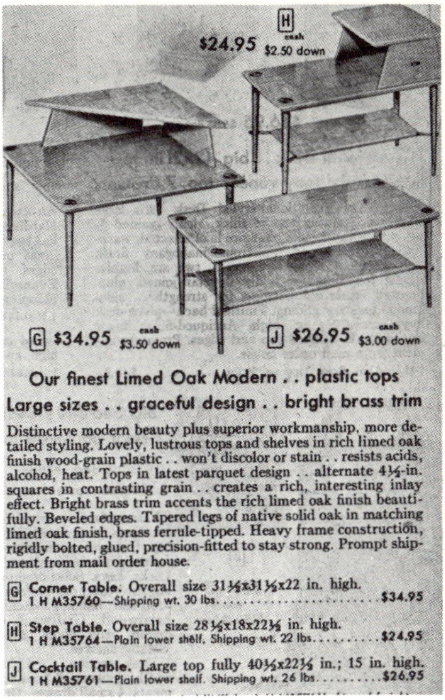

Copyright John H. Breck, Inc. ©
From the 1955 Sears, Roebuck and Co. catalog.

without ceasing to be a "nice girl?" Was America beginning to allow her favorite female image more liberty as long as she made the deliberate and conscious choice to become a blonde? Why is the artificial color change so openly recommended? What might this have to do with the enthusiastic acceptance of artificial materials like vinyl, particularly plastic textures that are clearly and proudly synthetic, with even plastic dishes like Melmac becoming the vogue?

Why might people want to buy furniture that reminds them of metal? Since it is surely not connotative of physical comfort, metal and synthetics must have seemed admirable in some way. How might sectional furniture, with its emphasis on individual parts, relate to the adulation of movie stars who are admired for very specific parts of their bodies? (Sectional furniture was known jokingly in the 1950s as "sexual furniture.") What about the interchangeability of parts, things, and people? Nearly any woman could become a blonde, if she wanted to, and could wear "falsies" as a part of her. The mixing of "natural" and "artificial" materials, with even their complete exchange of function, was the mode. With shades of Horatio Alger, anyone

The Bettman Archive, Inc.

TODAY'S CASUAL LIVING CALLS FOR THIS NEW SECTIONAL FURNITURE

because it's easy to arrange in any room . . it adds beauty of metallic-high lighted fabric . . and NOW Foam Latex seat cushions keep their neat look always because covers can't slip!

2-pc. Sectional (A) and (AA) $179.95 each $18.00 down, $12.00 monthly

3-piece Sectional Sofa A, B, C SHOWN IN COLOR ON FACING PAGE $299.95 each $30.00 down (Each piece may be bought separately if desired)

Now! For the first time—100% foam latex seat cushions with cord-welted seams that stay straight! That's because Sears exclusive process makes fabric adhere to foam latex. Our laboratory tests prove no more sliding or slipping, no more wavy seams. No other upholstered furniture we know of has this revolutionary new feature!

New textured rayon and cotton boucle covers highlighted by silver-color metallic threads. All pieces are same 28½-in. height and 33½-in. depth—easy to combine into groups.

Deep 5⅝-in. crown foam latex seat cushions are reversible. Sagless spring backs and bases, thickly cotton padded. Rubberized hair and cotton padded arms. Kiln-dried hardwood frames. **Leg finish** French (light) walnut with satin brass trim. Tailored at factory near Rushville, Ind. in color you select.

5 HH colors Ming blue with black, Frosty pink with black, Charcoal gray with black, med. Mint green with brown, Sunshine yellow with brown; also white with black or with brown. *State color.*

Tables shown on this and facing page. Seafoam (light beige) color plastic tops and light walnut finished hardwood legs. Plastic on ¾-in. hardwood tops can't discolor or stain . . resists heat, cigarette burns. Gleaming brass handles, leg trims. Easy to assemble. From mail order house.

[A] 1 H M53833F—**Left Section** with arm. 48¾ in. long. 41x21½-inch seat. Shpg. wt. 109 lbs. *State color*. $92.95

[AA] 1 H M53834F—**Right Section** with arm, as above. 92.95

[A][AA] 1 H MT5352F—**2-pc. Sectional.** Left and right sections above. Total length 96½ in. Shpg. wt. 218 lbs. $179.95

[B] 1 H M53838F—**Curved Center Section.** Forms 90° angle. 57x21½-in. seat. 70-in. long back. Shpg. wt. 131 lbs. $109.95

[C] 1 H M53836F—**Right bumper-end Section.** Rounded corner. 57¼x21½-in. seat. Wt. 110 lbs. *State color*. $109.95

1 H M53835F—**Left Bumper.** Same as above, not shown. 109.95

[A][C] 1 H MT5353F—**2-pc. Sectional.** Left section (A), right bumper (C). Total length 105½ in. Shpg. wt. 219 lbs. $194.95

[A][B][C] 1 H MT5363F—**3-pc. Sectional featured.** Left section, center section, right bumper. Wt. 350 lbs. *State color*. . $299.95

1 H MT53819F—**3-pc. Sectional** (not shown). Left bumper, center section, right section with arm. Shpg. wt. 350 lbs. *State color*. $299.95

[D] 1 H M53837F—**Armless Chair.** Use alone or with any section. 30¼x21¼-in. seat. Wt. 75 lbs. *State color*. $64.95

[E] 1 H M53831F—**Arm Chair.** 33½ in. long. 21½x20¾-in. seat. Shipping wt. 95 lbs. *State color*. $79.95

[F] 1 H M53830F—**Sofa.** Shown at left. 75½ in. long. 62¾x21½-in seat. Shpg. wt. 159 lbs. *State color*. $139.95

[E][F] 1 H MT5351F—**2-pc. Suite. Sofa (F) and Arm Chair (E)** in matching color. Shpg. wt. 254 lbs. *State color*. $209.95

2-pc. Suite: Sofa, Chair $209.95 each $21.00 down

Catalog No.	Style of Table	Size	Shpg. wt.	Price
[G] 1HM37500	Corner Table	29x29x23 in. high	30 lbs.	$34.95
[H] 1HM37501	Cocktail Table	45x19¾x15¾ in. high	25 lbs.	29.95
[J] 1H037506L	Tier Table	12, 18 and 24-in. diam. tiers, 30 in. high	25 lbs.	26.50
[K] 1HM37504	Step Table	28x16x22 in. high	25 lbs.	26.95
[L] 1HM37505	Round Cocktail	36-in. diam. 15 in. high	28 lbs.	29.95

The rooms at right have been completely furnished with merchandise from this catalog. See index for page numbers where accessories are sold. Colors match merchandise as closely as high speed printing permits

From the 1955 Sears, Roebuck and Co. catalog.

From the 1955 Sears, Roebuck and Co. catalog.

could become anything or anybody (it was at least his obligation to try—imagine the role–identity confusion!) The American virtues of practicality, technical know-how and self-improvement supported the democratic belief that anyone and everyone could become a blonde and could have things (only money was needed—and everyone had the opportunity to make money)! And the wonders of technology seemed to promise an unlimited amount of mass-produced, indestructible (because they were synthetic) goods to an acquisitive America.

Marilyn Monroe herself is quite clearly a self-made, put-together product—not only the hair color changes, the dismissal of her earlier life, with the sordid past and the ignored first marriage—but also her attempts at artistic and intellectual self-improvement (her much-publicized desires to become "educated," to read novels, and her acting lessons at the serious Actors Studio). "Marilyn came to be regarded by many as uniquely American. On the set of '**The Misfits**' the French photographer Henri Cartier-Bresson had observed to James Goode, 'She's American, and it's very clear that she is—she's very good that way—one has to be very local to be universal.' Cartier-Bresson was also to say, 'There's something extremely alert and vivid in her, an intelligence. It's her personality, it's a glance. It's something very tenuous, very vivid that disappears quickly, that appears again.' She was more representative of the country itself than any of her Hollywood peers. She was willful and created her own success. She was predisposed to any underdog, but often appeared to be riding herd over those closest to her. She was preeminently exportable, but almost never for the reasons she herself preferred."[41]

Yet there was no doubt that, although she might be self-created, she had endearing imperfections that the American public seemed to take to its heart. Perhaps the comfortably imperfect is more approachable and accessible than idealized perfection, which always seems to be found in a far-away situation. The real girl-next-door may be happily homely in some ways, and all the furniture at Sears may not be elegant, but it's at least reassuring to know these things are obtainable. And maybe it was just the old American love of the underdog. Monroe's famous walk was actually awkward and slightly bow-legged and this, instead of some svelte movie queen image, became her trademark.

> "But more often than not, there was no glamor to be found in her modeling career. 'Lower your smile,' Emmeline instructed her. A photographer who had been sent some photos of her had found a flaw in her appearance. Her nose was too long.
>
> Emmeline recalled that Norma Jean seemed puzzled and held up a profile shot as proof of the man's mistake. 'It's the shadow, dear,' Emmeline explained. 'There isn't enough upper lip between the end of your nose and your mouth.' And then she walked around Norma Jean, studying her face, holding her chin in her hand a moment, and nodding to herself.
>
> 'Try smiling with your upper lip drawn down.' Norma Jean's mouth quivered a little with the effort, but she managed to lower her smile a notch.
>
> '*There*! Now your smile keeps your nose in place. Just practice that tonight at home before a mirror.'
>
> Norma Jean was never to feel entirely secure with that smile. Years later, after stardom had come, her lips would still move uncertainly as she smiled, and the movement would become part of her style."[42] (from **Norma Jean**)

[41] From *Norma Jean* by Fred Lawrence Guiles. Copyright 1969 by Fred Lawrence Guiles. Used with permission of McGraw-Hill Book Company.

[42] From *Norma Jean* by Fred Lawrence Guiles. Copyright 1969 by Fred Lawrence Guiles. Used with permission of McGraw-Hill Book Company.

Perhaps because of the uncertain, nearly bumbling quality, her sexuality was seen as anything but sinister; people felt they knew her. Everyone called her Marilyn, from Carl Sandburg, her friend, to taxicab drivers, who would recognize her and say, "Hi, Marilyn." At the height of her stardom, walking alone in New York City late at night, she talked for an hour once with a policeman about things, about life with a capital L. People were, in short, more than familiar with her and who they thought she was. If nothing else, the nude calendar had assured everyone that she was very real.

But the other side of the coin of fame and special powers was quite evident, as Marilyn herself notes:

MARILYN LETS HER HAIR DOWN ABOUT BEING FAMOUS[43]

Ever since she was fired from **Something's Got To Give**, *Marilyn Monroe has kept an almost disdainful silence. As far as her troubles with 20th Century-Fox were concerned, she simply said she had been too sick to work–not willfully tardy and truant as the producer charged. While 20th Century and her lawyers were negotiating for her to resume work on the movie, Marilyn was thinking about broader aspects of her career–about the rewards and burdens of fame bestowed on her by fans who paid $200 million to see her films, about drives that impel her, about echoes in her present life of her childhood in foster homes. She thought about these out loud in a rare and candid series of conversations with LIFE Associate Editor Richard Meryman. As a camera caught the warmth and gusto of her personality, Marilyn's words revealed her own private view of Marilyn Monroe.*

Sometimes wearing a scarf and a polo coat and no make-up and with a certain attitude of walking, I go shopping–or just looking at people living. But then you know, there will be a few teen-agers who are kind of sharp and they'll say, "Hey, just a minute–you know who I think that is?" And then they'll start tailing me. And I don't mind. I realize some people want to see if you're real. The teen-agers, the little kids, their faces light up–they say "gee" and they can't wait to tell their friends. And old people come up and say, "Wait till I tell my wife." You've changed their whole day.

In the morning the garbage men that go by 57th Street when I come out the door say, "Marilyn, hi! How do you feel this morning?" To me it's an honor, and I love them for it. The workingmen–I'll go by and they'll whistle.

[43]"Marilyn Lets Her Hair Down," by Richard Meryman. *Life*, August 3, 1962, © 1962 Time Inc.

At first they whistle because they think, oh, it's a girl, she's got blond hair and she's not out of shape, and then they say, "Gosh, it's Marilyn Monroe!" And that has its—you know, those are the times it's nice, people knowing who you are and all of that, and feeling that you've meant something to them.

I don't know quite why, but somehow I feel they know that I mean what I do—both when I'm acting on the screen or when if I see them in person and greet them—that I really always do mean hello and how are you? In their fantasies they feel—Gee, it can happen to me!

But when you're famous you kind of run into human nature in a raw kind of way. It stirs up envy, fame does. People you run into feel that, well, who is she—who does she think she is, Marilyn Monroe? They feel fame gives them some kind of privilege to walk up to you and say anything to you, you know, of any kind of nature—and it won't hurt your feelings—like it's happening to your clothing. One time here I am looking for a home to buy and I stopped at this place. A man came out and was very pleasant, very cheerful, and said, "Oh, just a moment, I want my wife to meet you." Well, she came out and said, "Will you please get off the premises?"

You're always running into people's unconscious. Let's take some actors—or directors. Usually they don't say it to me, they say it to the newspapers because that's a bigger play. You know, if they're only insulting me to my face that doesn't make a big enough play because all I have to do is say, "See you around, like never." But if it's the newspapers, it's coast to coast and on around the world. I don't understand why people aren't a little more generous with each other. I don't like to say this, but I'm afraid there is a lot of envy in this business. The only thing I can do is I stop and think, "I'm all right but I'm not so sure about *them*!"

For instance, you've read there was some actor that once said about me that kissing me was like kissing Hitler. Well, I think that's *his* problem. If I have to do intimate love scenes with somebody who really has these kind of feelings toward me, then my fantasy can come into play. In other words, out with him, in with my fantasy. He was never there.

But one thing about fame is the bigger the people are or the simpler the people are, the more they are not awed by you! They don't feel they have to be offensive, they don't feel they have to insult you. You can meet Carl Sandburg and he is so pleased to meet you. He wants to know about you and you want to know about him. Not in any way has he ever let me down. Or else you can meet working people who want to know what is it like. You try to explain to them. I don't like to disillusion them and tell them it's sometimes nearly impossible. They kind of look toward you for something that's away from their everyday life. I guess you call that entertainment, a world to escape into, a fantasy.

Sometimes it makes you a little bit sad because you'd like to meet somebody kind of on face value. It's nice to be included in people's fantasies but you also like to be accepted for your own sake.

I don't look at myself as a commodity, but I'm sure a lot of people have. Including, well, one corporation in particular which shall be nameless. If I'm sounding picked on or something, I think I am. I'll think I have a few wonderful friends and all of a sudden, oooh, here it comes. They do a lot of things—they talk about you to the press, to their friends, tell stories, and you know, it's disappointing. These are the ones you aren't interested in seeing every day of your life.

Of course, it *does* depend on the people, but sometimes I'm invited places to kind of brighten up a dinner table—like a musician who'll play the piano after dinner, and I know you're not really invited for yourself. You're just an ornament.

When I was 5—I think that's when I started wanting to be an actress—I loved to play. I didn't like the world around me because it was kind of grim—but I loved to play house and it was like you could make your own boundaries. It goes beyond house—you could make your own situations and you could pretend and even if the other kids were a little slow on the imagining part you could say, "Hey, what about if you were such and such and I were such and such—wouldn't that be fun?" And they'd say, "Oh, yes," and then I'd say, "Well, that will be a horse and this will be—" it was play, playfulness. When I heard that this was acting, I said that's what I want to be—you can play. But then you grow up and find out about playing, that they make playing very difficult for you.

Some of my foster families used to send me to the movies to get me out of the house and there I'd sit all day and way into the night—up in front, there with the screen so big, a little kid all alone, and I loved it. I loved anything that moved up there and I didn't miss anything that happened—and there was no popcorn either.

When I was 11 the whole world which was always closed to me—I just felt like I was on the outside of the world—suddenly, everything opened up. Even the girls paid a little attention to me just because they thought, 'Hmmm, she's to be dealt with!" And I had this long walk to school—2 1/2 miles to school, 2 1/2 miles back—it was just sheer pleasure. Every fellow honked his horn—you know, workers driving to work, waving, you know, and I'd wave back. The world became friendly.

All the newspaper boys when they delivered the paper would come around to where I lived, and I used to hang from a limb of a tree, and I had sort of a sweatshirt on—I didn't realize the value of a sweatshirt in those days—and then I was sort of beginning to catch on, but I didn't quite get it because I couldn't really afford sweaters. But here they'd come with their bicycles, you know, and I'd get these free papers and the family liked that, and they'd all pull their bicycles up around the tree and then I'd be hanging, looking kind of like a monkey, I guess. I was a little shy to come down. I did get down to the curb, kinda kicking the curb and kicking the leaves and talking, but mostly listening.

And sometimes the families used to worry because I used to laugh so loud and so gay; I guess they felt it was hysterical. It was just this sudden freedom because I would ask the boys, "Can I ride your bike now?" And they'd say, "Sure." Then I'd go zooming, laughing in the wind, riding down the block, laughing, and they'd all stand around and wait till I came back, but I loved the wind. It caressed me.

But it was kind of a double-edged thing. I did find, too, when the world opened up that people took a lot for granted, like not only could they be friendly, but they could get suddenly overly friendly and expect an awful lot for very little.

When I was older, I used to go to Grauman's Chinese Theatre and try to fit my foot in the prints in the cement there. And I'd say, "Oh, oh, my foot's too big, I guess, that's out." I did have a funny feeling later when I finally put my foot down into that wet cement. I sure knew what it really meant to me—anything's possible, almost.

It was the creative part that kept me going—trying to be an actress. I enjoy acting when you really hit it right. And I guess I've always had too much fantasy to be only a housewife. Well, also, I had to eat. I was never kept, to be blunt about it. I always kept myself. I have always had a pride in the fact that I was on my own. And Los Angeles was my home, too, so when they said, "Go home!" I said, "I *am* home."

The time when I sort of began to think I was famous I was driving somebody to the airport and as I came back there was this movie house and I saw my name in lights. I pulled the car up at a distance down the street—it was too much to take up close, you know—all of a sudden. And I said, "God, somebody's made a mistake." But there it was, in lights. And I sat there and said, "So that's the way it looks," and it was all very strange to me, and yet at the studio they had said, "Remember you're not a star." Yet there it is up in lights.

I really got the idea I must be a star, or something, from the newspapermen—I'm saying men, not the women—who would interview me and they would be warm and friendly. By the way, that part of the press, you know, the men of the press, unless they have their own personal quirks against me, they were always very warm and friendly and they'd say, "You know, you're the only star," and I'd say, "star?" and they'd look at me as if I were nuts.

I think they, in their own kind of way, made me realize I was famous.

I remember when I got the part in **Gentlemen Prefer Blondes.** Jane Russell—she was the brunette in it and I was the blonde—she got $200,000 for it and I got my $500 a week, but that to me was, you know, considerable. She, by the way, was quite wonderful to me. The only thing was I couldn't get a dressing room. I said, finally—I really got to this kind of level—I said, "Look, after all, I am the blonde and it is **Gentlemen Prefer Blondes**!" Because still they always kept saying, "Remember, you're not a star." I said, "Well, whatever I am, I *am* the blonde!"

And I want to say that the people—if I am a star—the people made me a star—no studio, no person, but the people did. There was a reaction that came to the studio, the fan mail, or when I went to a premiere, or the exhibitors wanted to meet me. I didn't know why. When they all rushed toward me I looked behind me to see who was there and I said, "My heavens!" I was scared to death. I used to get the feeling, and sometimes I still get it, that sometimes I was fooling somebody. I don't know who or what—maybe myself.

I've always felt toward the slightest scene—even if all I had to do in a scene was just to come in and say, "Hi," that the people ought to get their money's worth and that this is an obligation of mine, to give them the best you can get from me. I do have feelings some days when there are some scenes with a lot of responsiblity towards the meaning and I'll wish, gee, if only I would have been a cleaning woman. On the way to the studio I would see somebody cleaning and I'd say, "That's what I'd like to be. That's my ambition in life." But I think all actors go through this. We not only *want* to be good; we have to be.

You know, when they talk about nervousness—my teacher, Lee Strasberg—when I said to him, "I don't know what's wrong with me but I'm a little nervous," he said, "When you're not, give up, because nervousness indicates sensitivity."

Also, a struggle with shyness is in every actor more than anyone can imagine. There is a censor inside us that says to what degree do we let go, like a child playing. I guess people think we just go out there, and you know, that's all we do—just do it. But it's a real struggle. I'm one of the world's most self-conscious people. I really have to struggle.

An actor is not a machine, no matter how much they want to say you are. Creativity has got to start with humanity and when you're a human being, you feel, you suffer—you're gay, you're sick, you're nervous or whatever. Like any creative human being, I *would* like a bit more control so that it would be a little easier for me when the director says, "One tear, right now," that one tear would pop out. But once there came two tears because I thought, "How dare he?"

Goethe said, "Talent is developed in privacy," you know? And it's really true. There is a need for aloneness which I don't think most people realize for an actor. It's almost having certain kinds of secrets for yourself that you'll let the whole world in on only for a moment, when you're acting.

But everybody is always tugging at you. They'd all like sort of a chunk of you. They kind of like take pieces out of you. I don't think they realize it, but it's like "rrrr do this, rrrr do that." But you do want to stay intact—intact and on two feet.

I think that when you are famous every weakness is exaggerated. This industry should behave like a mother whose child has just run out in front of a car. But instead of clasping the child to them, they start punishing the child. Like you don't dare get a cold—how dare you get a cold! I mean, the executives can get colds and stay home forever and phone it in, but how dare you, the actor, get a cold or a virus. You know, no one feels worse than the one who's sick. I sometimes wish, gee, I wish they had to act a comedy with a temperature and a virus infection. I am not an actress who appears at a studio just for the purpose of discipline. This doesn't have anything at all to do with art. I myself would like to become more disciplined within my work. But I'm there to give a performance and not to be disciplined by a studio! After all, I'm not in a military school. This is supposed to be an art form, not just a manufacturing establishment.

The sensitivity that helps me to act, you see, also makes me react. An actor is supposed to be a sensitive instrument. Isaac Stern takes good care of his violin. What if everybody jumped on his violin?

If you've noticed in Hollywood where millions and billions of dollars have been made, there aren't really any kind of monuments or museums, and I don't call putting your footprint in Grauman's Chinese a monument—alright this did mean a lot to sentimental bally-hoo me at the time. Gee, nobody left anything behind, they took it, they grabbed it and they ran—the ones who made the billions of dollars, never the workers.

You know a lot of people have, oh gee, real quirky problems that they wouldn't dare have anyone know. But one of my problems happens to show—I'm late. I guess people think that why I'm late is some kind of arrogance and I think it is the opposite of arrogance. I also feel that I'm not in this big American rush—you know, you got to go and you got to go fast but for no good reason. The main thing is, I do want to be prepared when I get there to give a good performance or whatever to the best of my ability.

A lot of people can be there on time and do nothing, which I have seen them do, and you know, all sit around and sort of chit-chatting and talking trivia about their social life. Gable said about me, "When she's there, she's there. All of her is there! She's there to work."

I was honored when they asked me to appear at the President's birthday rally in Madison Square Garden. There was like a hush over the whole place when I came on to sing *Happy Birthday*—like if I had been wearing a slip I would have thought it was showing, or something. I thought, "Oh, my gosh, what if no sound comes out!"

A hush like that from the people warms me. It's sort of like an embrace. Then you think, by God, I'll sing this song if it's the last thing I ever do. And for all the people. Because I remember when I turned to the microphone I looked all the way up and back and I thought, "That's where I'd be—way up there under one of those rafters, close to the ceiling, after I paid my $2 to come into the place."

Afterwards they had some sort of a reception. I was with my former father-in-law, Isadore Miller, so I think I did something wrong when I met the President. Instead of saying, "How do you do?" I just said, "This is my former father-in-law, Isadore Miller." He came here an immigrant and I thought this would be one of the biggest things in his life—he's about 75 or 80 years old and I thought this would be something that he would be telling his grandchildren about and all that. I should have said, "How do you do, Mr. President," but I had already done the singing, so well you know. I guess nobody noticed it.

Fame has a special burden, which I might as well state here and now. I don't mind being burdened with being glamorous and sexual. But what goes with it can be a burden—like the man was going to show me around but the woman said, "Off the premises." I feel that beauty and femininity are ageless and can't be contrived, and glamor—although the manufacturers won't like this—cannot be manufactured. Not real glamor, it's based on femininity. I think that sexuality is only attractive when it's natural and spontaneous. This is where a lot of them miss the boat. And then something I'd just like to spout off on. We are all born sexual creatures, thank God, but it's a pity so many people despise and crush this natural gift. Art, real art, comes from it—everything.

I never quite understood it—this sex symbol—I always thought symbols were those things you clash together! That's the trouble, a sex symbol becomes a thing. I just hate to be a thing. But if I'm going to be a symbol of something I'd rather have it sex than some other things they've got symbols of! These girls who try to be me—I guess the studios put them up to it, or they get the ideas themselves. But gee, they haven't—you can make a lot of gags about it—like they haven't got the foreground or else they haven't the background. But I mean the middle, where you live.

All my stepchildren carried the burden of my fame. Sometimes they would read terrible things about me and I'd worry about whether it would hurt them. I would tell them, don't hide these things from me. I'd rather you ask me these things straight out and I'll answer all your questions. Don't be afraid to ask anything. After all I have come up from way down.

I wanted them to know of lives other than their own. I used to tell them, for instance, that I worked for 5¢ a month and I washed one hundred dishes, and my stepkids would say, "One hundred dishes!" and I said, "Not only that, I scraped and cleaned them before I washed them. I washed them and rinsed them and put them in the draining place, but," I said, "thank God I didn't have to dry them." Kids are different from grownups—you know when you can get kind of sour, I mean that's the way it can go, but kids accept you the way you are.

I always tell them, "Don't admire somebody because they are grown up or because they say certain things—kind of observe them a little bit." I think probably that is the best advice I have given them. Just observe people for a while and then make up your own mind. And I used to tell them that about myself. I said, "See if I'm worth being a friend. That's up to you, and you figure it out after a while."

Fame to me certainly is only a temporary and a partial happiness—even for a waif and I was brought up a waif. But fame is not really for a daily diet, that's not what fulfills you. It warms you a bit but the warming is temporary. It's like caviar, you know—it's good to have caviar but not when you have to have it every meal and every day.

I was never used to being happy, so that wasn't something I ever took for granted. I did sort of think, you know, marriage did that. You see, I was brought up differently from the average American child because the average child is brought up expecting to be happy—that's it, successful, happy, and on time. Yet because of fame I was able to meet and marry two of the nicest men I'd ever met up to that time.

I don't think people will turn against me, at least not by themselves. I like people. The "public" scares me but people I trust. Maybe they can be impressed by the press or when a studio starts sending out all kinds of stories. But I think when people go to see a movie, they judge for themselves. We human beings are strange creatures and still reserve the right to think for ourselves.

Once I was supposed to be finished—that was the end of me. When Mr. Miller was on trial for contempt of Congress, a certain corporation executive said either he named names and I got him to name names, or I was finished. I said, "I'm proud of my husband's position and I stand behind him all the way," and the court did too. "Finished," they said. "You'll never be heard of."

It might be kind of a relief to be finished. It's sort of like I don't know what kind of a yard dash you're running, but then you're at the finish line and you sort of sigh—you've made it! But you never have—you have to start all over again. But I believe you're always as good as your potential.

I now live in my work and in a few relationships with the few people I can really count on. Fame will go by and, so long, I've had you, fame. If it goes by, I've always known it was fickle. So at least it's something I experienced, but that's not where I live.

Marilyn attributes the ambiguous attitude people have toward her fame and sexuality to their envy of her. Yet she also says, "You're always running into people's unconscious." Is it true, as Marilyn suggests, that there is something deeper and more primitive going on? Is it unfair to suggest that many people want to bring down those more gifted than they are or, more complexly, perhaps want to destroy the symbol or force that has liberated them from a previous, less desirable, but more structured and predictable state? One anthropological view states:

"Fourthly, the employment of a divine man or animal as a scapegoat is especially to be noted; indeed, we are here directly concerned with the custom of banishing evils only in so far as these evils are believed to be transferred to a god who is afterwards slain. It may be suspected that the custom of employing a divine man or animal as a public scapegoat is much more widely diffused than appears from the examples cited. For, as has already been pointed out, the custom of killing a god dates from so early a period of human history that in later ages, even when the custom continues to be practiced, it is liable to be misinterpreted. The divine character of the animal or man is forgotten, and he comes to be regarded merely as an ordinary victim. This is especially likely to be the case when it is a divine man who is killed. For when a nation becomes civilised, if it does not drop human sacrifices altogether, it at least selects as victims only such wretches as would be put to death at any rate. Thus the killing of a god may sometimes come to be confounded with the execution of a criminal.

If we ask why a dying god should be chosen to take upon himself and carry away the sins and sorrows of the people, it may suggested that in the practice of using the divinity as a scapegoat we have a combination of two customs which were at one time distinct and independent. On the one hand we have seen that it has been customary to kill the human or animal god in order to save his divine life from being weakened by the inroads of age. On the other hand we have seen that it has been customary to have a general expulsion of evils and sins once a year. Now, if it occurred to people to combine these two customs, the result would be the employment of the dying god as a scapegoat. He was killed, not originally to take away sin, but to save the divine life from the degeneracy of old age; but, since he had to be killed at any rate, people may have thought that they might as well seize the opportunity to lay upon him the burden of their sufferings and sins, in order that he might bear it away with him to the unknown world beyond the grave."[44]

Marilyn declares that, "We are all born sexual creatures, thank God, but it's a pity so many people despise and crush this natural gift. Art, real art, comes from it—everything." And the cultural analyst Diana Trilling assigns the same cause when she says that Monroe's gift of biology had the same sexual origins as that of any great artist. She explains Marilyn's destruction, however, as the inevitable, equalizing result of possessing one extraordinary gift; that the public's occasional bitterness towards her came from its own sexual confusion and restraining inhibitions, from which Marilyn was simultaneously and ironically freeing it.

THE DEATH OF MARILYN MONROE[45]

DIANA TRILLING

On a Sunday morning in August 1962, Marilyn Monroe, aged thirty-six, was found dead in the bedroom of her home in Los Angeles, her hand on the telephone as if she had just received, or, far more likely, been about to make a call. On the night table next to her bed stood a formidable array of medicines, among them a bottle that had held twenty-five Nembutal pills, now empty. Two weeks later a team of psychiatrists, appointed by the state in conformity with California law, brought in its report on the background and circumstances of her death, declaring it a suicide. There had of course never been any suggestion of foul play. The death was clearly self-inflicted, a climax of extended mental suffering. In fact, it was soon revealed that on Saturday evening Marilyn Monroe had made an emergency call to the psychoanalyst who had been treating her for her acute sleeplessness, her anxieties and depression, and that he had paid her a visit. But the formal psychiatric verdict had to do with the highly technical question of whether the overdose of barbiturates

[44] Excerpt from Sir James Frazier's *The Golden Bough* from the section "On Scapegoats in General". © 1922 Macmillan Co., © renewed with permission of Macmillan Publishing Co., Inc.

[45] "The Death of Marilyn Monroe" by Diana Trilling. Copyright, 1963, by Diana Trilling. Reprinted from her volume CLAREMONT ESSAYS, by permission of Harcourt Brace Jovanovich, Inc. (page 48 in ms.)

Marilyn "At the premiere of **The Seven Year Itch**, *1954".*
Through the Courtesy of Twentieth-Century Fox film Corporation.

was purposeful or accidental: had Marilyn Monroe *intended* to kill herself when she took the twenty-five sleeping pills? The jury of experts now ruled it was purposeful: she had wanted to die.

It is an opinion, or at least a formulation, that can bear, I believe, a certain amount of modification. Obviously, I'm not proposing that Marilyn Monroe's death was accidental in the sense that she took so large a dose of pills with no knowledge of their lethal properties. But I think it would be more precise to call this kind of death incidental rather than purposeful—incidental to the desire to escape the pain of living. I am not a psychiatrist and I never knew Marilyn Monroe, but it seems to me that a person can want to be released from consciousness without seeking actual death; that someone can want to stop living without wishing to die. And this is my feeling about Marilyn Monroe, that even when she had spoken of "wanting to die" she really meant that she wanted to end her suffering, not her life. She wanted to destroy consciousness rather than herself. Then, having taken the pills, she realized she might never return from the sleep she craved so passionately and reached for the phone for help.

But this is of course only speculation, and more appropriately engaged in by the medical profession than by the layman. For the rest of us, the motives surrounding Marilyn Monroe's suicide fade in importance before the all-encompassing reality of the act itself: Marilyn Monroe terminated her life. While the medical experts pondered the delicate difference between accident and suicide, the public recognized that the inevitable had at last occurred: Marilyn Monroe had killed herself. Shocked and grieved as everyone was, no one was at all surprised that she had died by her own hand, because for some years now the world had been prepared for just some such tragic outcome to one of the extraordinary careers of our time.

The potentiality of suicide or, at any rate, the threat of extreme mental breakdown had been, after all, conveyed to us by virtually every news story about Marilyn Monroe of recent years. I don't mean that it had been spelled out that she would one day take her life or otherwise go off the deep psychic end. But no one seemed able to write about her without reassuring us that despite her instability and the graveness of her emotional problems, she was still vital and eager, still, however precariously, a going concern. Marilyn Monroe was an earnest, ambitious actress, determined to improve her skill; Marilyn Monroe had failed in several marriages but she was still in pursuit of fulfillment in love; Marilyn Monroe had several times miscarried but she still looked forward to having children; Marilyn Monroe was seriously engaged in psychoanalysis; Marilyn Monroe's figure was better than ever; she was learning to be prompter; she was coping, or was struggling to cope, with whatever it was that had intervened in the making of her last picture—so, on the well-worn track, ran all the news stories. Even what may have been her last interview to appear in print (by the time it came out, she was already dead) sounded the same dominant chord of hopefulness, telling us of a Marilyn Monroe full of confidence that she would improve her acting and find her roles, and that between the two therapies, hard work and psychoanalysis, she would achieve the peace of mind that had for so long eluded her.

Where there is this much need for optimism, surely there is great peril, and the public got the message. But what is striking is the fact that throughout this period of her mounting difficulties, with which we were made so familiar, the popular image remained intact. Whatever we were told of her weak hold on life, we retained our image of Marilyn Monroe as the very embodiment of life energy. I think my response to her death was the common one: it came to me with the impact of a personal deprivation but I also felt it as I might a catastrophe in history or in nature; there was less in life, there was less of life, because she had ceased to exist. In her loss life itself had been injured.

In my own instance, it happens that she was already an established star before I knew her as anything except the latest pin-up girl. There is always this shield of irony some of us raise between ourselves and any object of popular adulation, and I had made my dull point of snubbing her pictures. Then one evening I chanced on a television trailer for **Bus Stop**, and there she was. I'm not even sure I knew whom I was seeing on the screen, but a light had gone on in the room. Where everything had been gray there was all at once an illumination, a glow of something beyond the ordinarily human. It was a remarkable moment, of a kind I don't recall having had with any other actress, and it has its place with certain rare, cherished experiences of art such as my youthful remembrance of Pavlova, the most perfect of performing artists, whose control of her body was like a radiance, or even the quite recent experience of seeing some photographs of Nijinsky in motion. Marilyn Monroe was in motion, too, which is important, since no still picture could quite catch her electric quality; in posed pictures the redundancy of flesh was what first imposed itself, dimming one's perception of its peculiar aliveness, of the translucence that infused body with spirit. In a moment's flash of light, the ironies with which I had resisted this sex idol, this object of an undifferentiating public taste, dropped from me never to be restored.

But mine was a minority problem; the world had long since recognized Marilyn Monroe's unique gift of physical being and responded to it as any such gift of life demands. From the start of her public career it had acknowledged the genius of biology or chemistry or whatever it was that set this young woman apart from the general kind. And once it had admitted her magic, nothing it was to learn of her "morbidity" could weigh against the conviction that she was alive in a way not granted the rest of us, or, more accurately, that she communicated such a charge of vitality as altered our imagination of life, which is of course the whole job and wonder of art.

Since her death it has occurred to me that perhaps the reason we were able to keep these two aspects in which we knew Marilyn Monroe—her life affirmation and her impulse to death—in such discreet balance was that they never presented themselves to us as mutually exclusive but, on the contrary, as two intimately related, even expectable, facets of her extraordinary endowment. It is as if the world that loved Marilyn Monroe understood that her superabundant biology had necessarily to provoke its own restraint, that this is the cruel law by which nature, or at least nature within civilization, punishes those of us who ask too much of life or bring too much to life. We are told that when one of the senses is defective, nature frequently provides a compensation in another of the senses; the blind often hear better than the seeing, or have a sharper sense of touch. What we are not told but perhaps understand nonetheless is the working of nature's system of negative compensation—the price we pay for gift, the revenge that life seems so regularly to take upon distinction. Certainly our awareness of the more, the plus, in Marilyn Monroe prepared us for some sort of minus. The fact that this young woman whose biological gift was so out of the ordinary was in mental pain seemed to balance the ledger. And one can speculate that had we not known of her emotional suffering, we would have been prepared for some other awful fate for her—an airplane disaster, maybe, or a deforming illness. So superstition may be thought of as an accurate reading of the harder rules of life.

And yet it is difficult to suppose the gods could be all that jealous. Had Marilyn Monroe not been enough punished in childhood to ensure her against further misfortune? Once this poor forlorn girl had been so magically brought into her own, the most superstitious of us had the right to ask happiness for her ever after. It was impossible to think of Marilyn Monroe except as Cinderella. The strange power of her physical being seemed best explained and justified by the extreme circumstances of her early life—the illegitimate birth, the mad mother, the orphanage and near-mad foster homes, the rape by one of her early guardians. If there was no good fairy in Marilyn Monroe's life and no Prince Charming, unless Hollywood, this didn't rob her story of its fairy-book miraculousness; it merely assimilated to the old tale our newer legend of the self-made hero or heroine. Grace Kelly had had her good Philadelphia family to pave her path and validate her right to a crown. But Marilyn Monroe reigned only by virtue of her beauty and her determination to be raised out of the squalor and darkness, and to shine in the full, the fullest, light. It is scarcely a surprise that the brighter her radiance, the more we listened for the stroke of midnight that would put a limit on such transcendence.

But it was not only the distance Marilyn Monroe had traveled from her unhappy beginnings that represented for us a challenge of reality, to be punished by reality. If her gift is to be regarded not as that of the stage or screen, which I think it primarily was not, but as the gift of biology, she was among those who are greatly touched with power; she was of the true company of artists. And her talent was so out of the range of the usual that we were bound to feel of it that it was not to be contained in society as we know it; therefore it proposed its own dissolution. Like any great artistic gift, Marilyn Monroe's power of biology was explosive, a primitive and savage force. It had, therefore and inevitably, to be a danger both to herself and to the world in which it did its work. All art is fierce in the measure that it matters, finally, and in its savagery it chooses either to push against society, against the restrictions that hedge it in, or against the artist himself. And no doubt it is the incapacity of most human beings to sustain this inordinate pressure that accounts for the fact that the artist is an exception in any civilized population. To mediate between the assault upon oneself and upon society, to keep alive in the battle and come out more or less intact, is a giant undertaking in which the native endowment of what we call talent is probably but a small element.

Among the very few weapons available to the artist in this monstrous struggle, naiveté can be the most useful. But it is not at all my impression that Marilyn Monroe was a naive person. I think she was innocent, which is very different. To be naive is to be simple or stupid on the basis of experience, and Marilyn Monroe was far from stupid; no one who was stupid could have been so quick to turn her wit against herself, or to manage the ruefulness with which she habitually replied to awkward questioning. To be innocent is to suffer one's experience without being able to learn self-protection from it; as if will-lessly, innocence is at the mercy of experience, unable to mobilize counterforces to fortune.

Of Ernest Hemingway, for example, I feel much as I do of Marilyn Monroe, that he was unable to marshal any adequate defense against the painful events of his childhood, and this despite his famous toughness and the courage he could call upon in war, in hunting, in all the dangerous enterprises that seduced him. He was an innocent man, not a naive man, though not always intelligent. Marilyn Monroe offers us a similar paradox. Even while she symbolized an extreme of experience, of sexual knowingness, she took each new circumstance of life, as it came to her or as she sought it, like a newborn babe. And yet this was what made her luminous—her innocence. The glow was not rubbed off her by her experience of the ugliness of life because finally, in some vital depth, she had been untouched by it.

From the psychiatrist's point of view, too much innocence, a radical disproportion between what has happened to a person and what he has absorbed from his experience, is a symptom, and alarming. It can indicate a rude break in his connection with himself, and if he is in treatment, it suggests a difficult cure, since, in emotional logic, he will probably be as impervious to the therapy as to the events through which he has passed, and yet without any mitigation of suffering. In the creative spheres, an excess of innocence unquestionably exercises an enormous fascination on us; it produces the purity of expression which leads us to say of an artistic creation or performance that it is "out of this world." But the psychiatric judgment has to pick its way on tiptoe between the gift and the pathology. What constitutes a person's art may eventually spell his emotional undoing.

I can suppose of Marilyn Monroe that she was peculiarly elusive to the psychiatrists or analysts who tried to help her, that emotionally speaking she presented herself to them as a kind of blank page on which nothing had been written, failing to make the connection between herself and them even as she pleaded for it. And yet disconnection was at the heart of her gift, it defined her charm for the world, much as Hemingway's dissociation from his own experience was determinative of his gift.

For several decades, scores of writers have tried to imitate Hemingway's style: the flexibility and purity of his prose, the bright, cogent distance he was able to put between himself and the object under examination. But none has succeeded. And I believe this is because his prose was, among many other things, a direct report of the unbridgeable distance between external reality and his emotions. Just so, Marilyn Monroe was inimitable. Hollywood, Broadway, the night clubs: they all regularly produce their quota of sex queens, but the public takes them and leaves them, or doesn't really take them; the world is not enslaved as it was by Marilyn Monroe because none but Marilyn Monroe could suggest such a purity of sexual delight. The boldness with which she could parade herself and yet never be gross, her sexual flamboyance and bravado which yet breathed an air of mystery and even reticence, her voice which carried such ripe overtones of erotic excitement and yet was the voice of a shy child—these complications were integral to her gift. And they described a young woman trapped in some never-never land of unawareness.

What I imply here, of course, is a considerable factitiousness in Marilyn Monroe as a sexual figure. Certainly the two or three men I've known who met her in "real life" were agreed on her lack of direct sexual impact; she was sweet and beautiful and lovely, yes, but somehow not at all the arousing woman they had expected. The nature of true sexuality is most difficult to define, so much of what we find sexually compelling has its source in phantasies that have little to do with the primary sexual instinct. Especially in the case of a movie star we enter a realm where dream and biology make their easiest merger. The art of acting is the art of *performing as if*, and the success of this feat of suggestion depends upon the degree to which it speaks to some phantasy of the onlookers

Marilyn Monroe spoke to our dreams as much as to our animal nature, but in a most unusual way. For what she appealed to was our determination to be rid of phantasy and to get down to the rock-bottom actuality. She gratified our wish to confront our erotic desires without romance, without diversion. And working within a civilization like ours, in which sexuality is so surrounded with restraints and fears and prohibitions, she perhaps came as close as possible to giving us the real thing. But she didn't give us the real thing; she merely acted as if she were giving it to us. She glamorized sexuality to the point at which it lost its terrors for us; and maybe it was this veil that she raised to sexual reality that permitted women, no less than men, to respond to her so generously. Instinctively, I think, women understood that this seemingly most sexual of female creatures was no threat to them.

The myth of Marilyn Monroe was thus even more of a myth than we realized, for this girl who was supposed to release us from our dreams into sexual actuality was in all probability not actual even to herself. Least of all could she have been sexually actual to herself and at the same time such a marvelous public performer of sex, such a conscious artist of sex. And we can conjecture that it was this deep alienation from her own feelings, including her sexual feeling, that enabled her to sustain the disorder of her early years even as long and as well as she did, and to speak of her awful childhood so simply and publicly. For most of us, the smallest "shame" in our past must be kept locked from others. We prefer that the least menacing of skeletons remain in the closet lest our current image of ourselves be violated by its emergence into the open. But Marilyn Monroe had no need for such reserves. She told the public the most gruesome facts of her personal history, for all the world as if we on the outside were worthy of such confidences-except that in some odd, generous response to her innocence, we exceeded ourselves in her instance and didn't take the advantage of her that we might have. Judged from the point of view of what we require of the artist, that he have the will and fearlessness to rise above the conventions which bind those of us with less gift, Marilyn Monroe's candor about her early life was something to be celebrated. But from another point of view her frankness was a warning that the normal barriers of self-protection were down or nonexistent, leaving her grievously exposed to the winds of circumstance.

And indeed the very word "exposed" is a key word in the pattern of her life. She was an actress and she exposed her person and her personality to the public gaze. She was an exposed human being who told the truth about herself too readily, too publicly. And more than most actresses, she exposed her body, with but inadequate understanding of what this involved. We recall, for instance, the awkward little scandal about her having once posed naked for a calendar and the bewildered poise, the really untoward innocence and failure of comprehension, with which she met the dismay of her studio, as if to say, "But that was me yesterday when I needed money. That isn't me today; today I have money." Just as today and yesterday were discontinuous with each other, she was discontinuous with herself, held together, one feels, only and all too temporarily by her success.

And this success was perhaps more intimately connected with her awareness of her physical appeal than we always understood. It may well have been the fact that she was so much and so admiringly in the public eye that gave Marilyn Monroe the largest part of her sense of a personal identity. Not long before her death, we now discover, she had herself photographed in the nude, carefully editing the many pictures as if to be certain she left the best possible record for posterity. The photographs leave, however, a record only of wasted beauty, at least of the famous body—while Marilyn Monroe's face is lovely as ever, apparently unscarred by her intense suffering, her body looked ravaged and ill, already drained of life. Recently the pictures have been published in an expensive magazine devoted to erotica. If their high price, prohibitive to the general buyer, could be interpreted as a precaution against their being too easily available to a sensation-seeking audience, the restraint was not really necessary. At the last, the nude Marilyn Monroe could excite no decent viewer to anything but the gentlest pity, and much fear.

But even before this ultimate moment the public success had been threatened. The great career was already failing. There had not been a Marilyn Monroe movie for a long time, and the last film she had worked on had had to be halted because she was unable to appear. And there was no private life to fall back upon, not even the formal structure of one: no marriage, no family, apparently not even friends. One had come, indeed, to think of her as the loneliest of people, so that it was not without bitterness that, on her death, one discovered that it was not only oneself who had wished to help her but many other strangers, especially women to whose protectiveness her extreme vulnerability spoke so directly. But we were the friends of whom she knew nothing, and among the people she knew it would seem that real relationships were out of reach across the desert emptiness that barricades whoever is out of touch with his feelings. One thinks of her that last evening of her life, alone and distraught, groping for human comfort and finding nothing but those endless bottles of medicine, and one confronts a pathos worse than tragedy.

Certainly it strains justice as well as imagination that the world's most glamorous woman should have been alone, with no date, on a Saturday night—for it was, in fact, a Saturday night when she killed herself. On other nights but Saturday, we are allowed our own company. Saturday night is when all American boys and girls must prove themselves sexually. This is when we must be "out," out in the world where we can be seen among the sexually chosen. Yet the American girl who symbolized sexual success for all of us spent her last Saturday night alone in despair. Every man in the country would have wanted to date Marilyn Monroe, or so he would say, but no man who knew her did.

Or, contemplating her loneliness, we think of her funeral, which, contrived to give her the peace and privacy that had so strenuously eluded her throughout her life, yet by its very restraint and limited attendance reminded us of the limitations of her actual connection with the world. Joe DiMaggio, who had been her husband for a few brief months earlier in her career, was the chief mourner. It was DiMaggio to whom, she had told us, it was impossible to be married because he had no conversation; at meals, instead of talking to her, he read the papers or looked at television. The more recent husband, *with* conversation, was not present, no doubt for his own inviolable reasons, but it was saddening. I do not know what, if anything, was read at the service, but I'd like to think it was of an elevated and literary kind, such as might be read at the funeral of a person of the first intellectual rank.

For of the cruelties directed at this young woman even by the public that loved her, it seems to me that the most biting, and unworthy of the supposedly enlightened people who were particularly guilty of it, was the mockery of her wish to be educated, or thought educated. Granting our right to be a bit confused when our sex idol protests a taste for Dostoevsky, surely the source of our discomfort must yet be located in our suspicions of Dostoevsky's worth for us and in our own sexual unease rather than in Marilyn Monroe. For what our mockery signifies is our disbelief that anyone who has enough sexuality needs to read Dostoevsky. The notion that someone with Marilyn Monroe's sexual advantages could have wanted anything except to make love robbed us of a prized illusion, that enough sexual possibility is enough everything.

I doubt that sex was enough anything for Marilyn Monroe, except the means for advancing herself in the world. One of the touching revelations of her early life was her description of how she discovered that somehow she was sexually different from other girls her age: the boys all whistled at her and crowded to her like bears to honey, so she came to realize that she must have something special about her, which she could use to rise above her poor circumstances. Her sexual awareness, that is, came to her from outside herself. It would be my guess that it remained outside her always, leaving a great emptiness, where a true sexuality would have supplied her with a sense of herself as a person with connection and content.

This void she tried to fill in every way available, with wordly goods, with fame and public attention and marriage, and also in ways that turned out to be unavailable, like children and domesticity—nothing could be more moving than the eagerness with which she seized upon a Jewish mother-in-law, even upon Jewish ceremonials and cooking, as if in the home life of her last husband's people she would find the secret of emotional plenitude. She also tried to fill her emptiness with books and learning. How mean-spirited can we be, to have denied her whatever might have added to her confidence that she was really a solid person and not just an uninhabited body?

And that she had the intellectual capacity for education there can be no question, had it but been matched with emotional capacity. No one without a sharp native intelligence could have spoofed herself as gracefully as she did or parried reporters with such finesse. If we are to judge by her interviews, she was as singularly lacking in the endemic offstage dullness of actors and actresses, the trained courtesy and charm that is only another boring statement of their self-love, as she was deficient in the established defenses of her profession: one recalls no instance of even implied jealousy of her colleagues or of censure of others—directors, script-writers, husbands—for her own failures. Her generosity of spirit, indeed, was part of the shine that was on her. But unfortunately it spared everyone but herself; she had never studied self-justification. To herself she was not kind. She made fun of herself and of all that she had to go on in life: her biology. Certainly this added to her lovableness but it cut from under her the little ground that she could call her own. When she exhibited her sexual abundance with that wonderful, gay exaggeration of hers, or looked wide-eyed upon the havoc she wrought, it was her way of saying, "Don't be afraid. I don't take myself seriously so you don't have to take me seriously either." Her talent for comedy, in other words, was a public beneficence but personal depredation, for, far more than most people, she precisely needed the assurance that she weighed in the scheme of human life, that she had substance and reality, that she had all the qualifications that make for a person we take seriously. Herself a supplicant, she gave us comfort. Herself a beggar, she distributed alms.

At her death, several writers of good will who undertook to deal with the tragedy of her suicide blamed it on Hollywood. In the industry that had made millions from her and in the methods by which Hollywood had exploited her, they found the explanation of her failed life; they wrote about her as the sacrificial lamb on the altar of American vulgarity and greed. I share their disgust with Hollywood and I honor their need to isolate Marilyn Monroe from the nastiness that fed on her, but I find it impossible to believe that this girl would have been an iota better off were Hollywood to have been other than what we all know it to be, a madness in our culture.

The self-destructiveness that Marilyn Monroe carried within her had not been put there by the "system," however overbearing in its ugliness. Just as her sweetness was her own, and immune to the influences of Hollywood, her terrors were also her own. They were not implanted in her though undoubtedly they were increased, by the grandiosity of being a star. Neither for better nor worse, I feel, was she essentially falsified or distorted by her public role, though she must often have suffered cruelly from the inescapability of the public glare. In fact, it would be my conjecture that had she never gone into the movies and become rich and world-famous, her troubled spirit would long since have had its way with her. She would have been equally undone, and sooner, and with none of the many alleviations and compensations that she must have known in these years of success.

This doesn't mean that I don't think she was a "victim." But she was not primarily a victim of Hollywood commercialism, or exploitation, or of the inhumanity of the press. She was not even primarily a victim of the narcissistic inflation that so regularly attends the grim business of being a great screen personality. Primarily she was a victim of her gift, a biological victim, a victim of life itself. It is one of the excesses of contemporary thought that we like to blame our very faulty culture for tragedies that are inherent in human existence—at least, inherent in human existence in civilization. I think Marilyn Monroe was a tragedy of civilization, but this is something quite else again from, and even more poignant than, being a specifically American tragedy.

As everyone now knows, the 1950s was the era of affluence and abundance. Never-ending progress *was* the most important product, and fin tails on cars and sprawling ranch-style houses made everyone perfectly sure that more than enough was never too much.

> "Miami Beach, with three quarters of its beach front already occupied by hotels, recently got its biggest and costliest addition, the $15 million Fontainebleau. A 14-story edifice with a 1000-foot beach, the hotel has 565 rooms (minimum $33 a day without meals). There are nine governor's suites (at $160 a day), nine presidential suites (at $185 a day) and a royal suite which will be even more expensive when finished. Fontainebleau has some striking architecture, two swimming pools, 265 cabanas and a million-dollar boiler room. Some of the first guests found the hotel's outsized magnificence almost overwhelming. But the management has a staff of 850 or roughly one employee for each guest, and expects in time 'everyone will feel like he is being carried around on his own little silver plate.' "[46]

[46] Excerpt from "Miami's Costliest Hotel." Copyright *Life*, January 17, 1955.

Photo of Cadillac by GM Photographic, Detroit, Michigan.

Photo of Marilyn Monroe by Culver Pictures.

Collage of two photos from LIFE'S January 17, 1955 article "Miami's Costliest Hotel." One of Fontainbleau, and one of the swimming facilities.

"A dramatically built staircase swoops up to the second tier of cabanas near ocean's edge." Photo from same Life January 17, 1955 article. Copyright Life magazine.

Curves and fullness expand upward in size and still keep going up to bigger and better goals. The fullness of 1940s expectations takes on qualities of exaggeration in the 1950s that provide not only the security of surplus material goods, but also the familiar American predilection for largeness and expansiveness. The financial security of the 1950s encouraged the ultimate Americana of "the more the merrier," of adding to your ranch or to your property. The smallest-size soapbox one could buy was the Big size, and of course King, Super, and Giant, were, and still are, the best possible sizes.

A progress line—future-seeking and -seeing—has always been the analogue for America: going westward, forgetting the European past, moving to another town; always with the prospect of a more rewarding life. And in the stringent

1930s perhaps this Dream was frustrated—the myth-fulfillment for it was an austere, apart woman. Her sexuality ambiguous, her appeal rested on removal rather than on connective involvement. In a Chinese puzzle of sexual invitational and frankness locked in with absolute inaccessibility, the American public knew what it wanted—just as it knew what material things it wanted—yet the beautiful despair and final denial provided the desire-frustration stalemate appropriate to hard times. In the next decade, however, the dream-myth found another form—things just might be realizable, both materially and sexually, once the war was over and once goods and women became possessable realities, as the 1940s developed. But for the time being in the 1940s, the carrot was still pretty far in front of the donkey; day-to-day living offered only a superficial excursion into the incredibly lavish setting and woman of dreams.

But when the 1950s happened, the material, "things" dream seemed realizable for everyone. And eventually so did the woman-sex dream, even if apparent wholesomeness and all-American blonde innocence was the vehicle. Hayworth may never be obtainable for the average guy in an ordinary setting and, certainly, Garbo never is, but Monroe is approachable and accessible. There can be no doubt that she is a realized, sexual being on *and* off the screen.

The trouble came perhaps when the things and the persons dream got mixed up. The fulfilled dream became a horrible nightmare for America: with finally attained goods people thought only of getting more (often of the same) and bigger goods. And with the realized sexual myth, all America could do, apparently, was imitate. Contrary to Monroe's own statement about naturalness, when it was all brought home, more and exaggerated, bosoms and blondeness was its dream enactment. And what was not *really* there could be "fixed" by the material stuff; it seemed only fair, after all. Perhaps this is how the mix-up occurred: the actualized dream becomes acted out only as a repetition and enlargement of someone else's artificially constructed dream-image (thus resulting in conformity, plasticity, and hypocrisy). And, as Monroe foresensed and foreacted the emerging sexuality, perhaps she also sensed the coming awareness of the emptiness of fabricated image-myth. Just daringly real enough to free us, she was perhaps American enough to devise, develop, and enlarge what might be embryonically there; and yet was intelligent enough to know that repeating and increasing some nonreal self might be suicidal (what suburbia and the discovery of anxiety revealed in perhaps more sordid ways).

The dream-myths of the 1960s and 1970s seem to have more diverse types: many old motifs are repeated but America no longer seems to settle on one particular goddess-type to reflect its psychic cravings. The sex queens are varied, and no one dominates the public consciousness: Raquel Welch, Ann-

Margret; even more popular European stars: Brigitte Bardot, Sophia Loren, Julie Christie, Vanessa Redgrave, and Elke Sommer. Frank sexuality they all have in common, but no strong mystique surrounds any one of them. Does America have no need for a uniform sex symbol now that film censorship is virtually nonexistent? Or is it that a sharply fragmented America can produce no mass consciousness and can agree on no universal symbol? For instance, how would race-proud minority groups respond to the adulation of blondeness, how would women's liberation groups deal with the admiration for *parts* of a woman's body or the pedestal-placing romanticization of some women and the "bad girl" qualities of other women?

Is the goddess-myth idea in general a valid one? Is the cultism a cathartic or an inhibiting factor for the public, or is it simply reflective of the idealized qualities already present in feminine types in the society? Is it based on the notion that you can never have what you really want or admire? Thus, after the nearly-tangible Monroe has made her gift of sexuality, there are many "real" stars, but few are overwhelmingly glamorous or exciting. Does this adoration of only the "unhaveable" reveal some sort of masochism in the American character or, perhaps, just a revival of Puritan self-denial? How closely might this tie in with the Western European tradition of courtly love, where the extreme of passion is stimulated by admiration for a woman who must, by definition, be out of reach or belong to someone else? Great love themes—Tristan and Isolde, Dante and Beatrice, and Lancelot and Guinevere—are always based on impossibility. And if Western man assumes that he can't have what he thinks he wants, what does this say about how he feels about what he does have? The woman or his dreams can never be the woman he can have and, naturally, the woman he has can never be the woman of his dreams.

The transmutation of all this may seem a bit weird in America, where the acquisition of your goal is an integral part of the American character. Yet denial and removal work well with the goddess myth. So accessibility and possession might have proved somewhat confusing and might have destroyed the inclination for adulation. Once you have it, repreating it and blowing it up, loving especially the synthetic parts, perhaps you begin to wonder about a possible hollowness inside and, hence, that something is radically wrong with mass-production, conformity, and massive acquisition of things. The fulfillment of the denied, removed dream seems to lead to the great soul searching of the self-critical and criticized America of the 1960s and 1970s; the dream itself was more loved and loveable than what has been done in the name of the realized dream.

1950s QUESTIONS AND PROJECTS

1. Pretend you are a movie star agent and construct a resumé (physical and type description) for a movie star that would appeal to various groups in America today; a star for the "counter-culture," for militant American Indian, Puerto Rican, black, or radical women's liberation groups, for backlash George Wallace-type people, for "middle America" (if you can define it), for example. And write a rationale to present to the studio's business office about why you think this particular star would "sell" to this certain audience.
2. Compare a 1951 or 1952 movie on television with one from 1958 or 1959, with the same basic plot in each. What changes in language, characterization, and attitudes have developed? What are the typical teenagers like in the two sets of 1950s films? Make a list of adjectives describing them, and compare with adjectives describing young people in current films.
3. Look at styles of clothing for men in the 1950s and compare with the large diversity of styles today. Note that the text of clothing advertisements changes from touting discrimination, good taste, and being clean-cut; to advice to break free, to express *yourself,* and to do your own thing. Brush cuts are the same on every person in the 1950s ads—how about the longer hair in contemporary ads?
4. Make lists, collages or montages of textures and materials that were popular in the 1930s, 1940s and 1950s. What do these tell you about the respective decades?
5. Read popular novels and fiction in pulp magazines of the 1950s, and try to determine whether eye and hair colors, body types, and other physical features are related to certain female-type characterizations.
6. Compare advertisements from the three decades and note the change in psychological sales appeal: from necessities, corner-cutting economic measures, to promises that companies are working on better things, to injunctions on buying now—why not. Then look at current ads. Make a graph of economic security for the past 45 years or so. Probably 1929 would be the beginning high point, with a dramatic drop.

7. Find comic books from the 1950s and catalogue the characters. Compare them with types from 1940s comics. Which characters are more "ordinary" and comfortably recognizable? When things are "brought home," how does fantasy operate? What form does violence take then?

8. To what extent is the sexual freedom on the screen in the 1950s, 1960s, and 1970s actually a reflection of what goes on in most American lives? Attempt a chart with two lines: one indicating repression-freedom in the films, the other contrasting one showing the relation to "reality."

9. Some people believe the goddess cult is over and done with in America, to be replaced by the adoration of other kinds of public personalities. Validate or disprove this theory by giving some examples of current mythologized figures.

10. Find a dress or outfit your mother wore in the 1950s, or look for one at a Salvation Army outlet. What do you make of exaggerated bosoms, small waists made possible by a combination of cinch belts, puffy skirts, and petticoats? What, for example, does all this say about the 1950s, its extremes, and natural shapes?